101 WAYS
TO GO
ZERO WASTE

101 WAYS TO GO ZERO WASTE

KATHRYN KELLOGG

THE COUNTRYMAN PRESS

A division of W. W. Norton & Company

Independent Publishers Since 1923

For my grandmother, Nina Jones

For information about permission to reproduce selections from this book, write to
Permissions, The Countryman Press, 500 Fifth Avenue, New York, NY 10110

For information about special discounts for bulk purchases, please contact
W. W. NortonSpecial Sales at specialsales@wwnorton.com or 800-233-4830

Manufacturing by LSC Communications, Harrisonburg
Book design by Chris Welch
Production manager: Devon Zahn

The Countryman Press
www.countrymanpress.com

A division of W. W. Norton & Company, Inc.
500 Fifth Avenue, New York, NY 10110
www.wwnorton.com

978-1-68268-331-6 (pbk.)

10 9 8 7 6

CONTENTS

INTRODUCTION
THE ZERO-WASTE MOVEMENT

Have you ever thought about your trash? Take a second and do it now. Think about what you throw away every day. Think about your trash both in and out of the home. Do you get a daily take-away coffee cup? Are you constantly tossing packaging materials from online purchases? Is your pantry filled with single-use food items? Now, ask yourself, "Where does all that trash go?" Have you thought about what happens after it leaves your curbside bin? It doesn't magically vanish after it leaves; it goes to a landfill. But, what if there was more to the story?

Consider all of the resources that go into producing the products we buy and all of the packaging that comes with them. When we truly think about all of the stuff we interact with, it becomes clear that some of the best things we can do are buy less, buy consciously, and produce as little waste as possible. The ultimate goal: zero waste.

What's the Problem?

According to the EPA, the average American sends 4.4 pounds of trash to the landfill every day. We live in a convenience-based society where we often believe that all our problems can be solved with cheap, disposable products destined for the landfill. On average, a piece of clothing is worn 7 times before being discarded, and plastic bags are only used for 15 minutes. "Convenience" items like coffee cups and paper towels use valuable resources, and our resource supply is finite. There is only so much the Earth can produce. Each year, Earth Overshoot Day marks the point at which we've consumed all of the resources the earth can sustainably produce for the year. In 2018, Earth Overshoot Day was August 1, 2018. We're essentially consuming 1.5 earths in a year's time.

Beyond our overconsumption problem, landfills themselves are toxic. They're responsible for 16 percent of methane emissions in the US, and methane is 30 percent more powerful than average greenhouse gases like CO_2. Because landfills aren't aerated for proper decomposition of organic material, the organic matter is stuck in limbo, releasing methane into the atmosphere. Furthermore, toxins from cleaners, batteries, small electronics, and other items that shouldn't be landfilled leach into the soil and can run off into the ocean and groundwater when it rains.

A lot of trash doesn't even make it to the landfill. Instead, it clutters the sides of roads and swirls in the ocean. There are five major gyres in the ocean which are essentially floating landfills. According to the Ellen MacArthur Foundation, there's expected to be more plastic than fish by 2050. Plastic is especially dangerous because it doesn't biodegrade; it photodegrades, which means it gets smaller and smaller, but never goes away. Plastic breaks down so small that according to a recent study by Orb Media, it's been found in drinking water worldwide with a staggering 94 percent rate in the US. Bottled water tested positive too, so don't think drinking bottled water is the solution—it's antagonizing the problem.

But I Recycle!

Recycling is great, but unfortunately it is not enough. There's simply too much recycling to process, and we're still consuming way too many resources. Recycling isn't a perfect solution. While it plays into the solution, we have to lessen our dependence on it. Did you know only 9 percent of all plastic is actually recycled? Recycling plants in the US don't process a lot of the materials we send them. Instead, they bale our recyclables and ship them to China. But at the start of 2018, China stopped accepting paper and plastic with a 1 percent contamination rate or higher. To put this in perspective, the best recycling facilities in the US are currently operating at 4 percent contamination level. Contamination occurs when incorrect materials are placed in the bale, or when there's a substance left on the materials, like food residue in a plastic tub or grease on paper. We can easily solve these problems by recycling better! See my guide to recycling like a boss on page 10.

Due to this current recycling crisis, we can expect to see the recycling rate of plastic drop even lower than it is already. Unlike steel, aluminum, and glass, plastic can't truly be recycled. You can't take a plastic water bottle, melt it down, and turn it into a new plastic water bottle. The material loses quality, and it has to be made into a different product like carpet or a fleece jacket. And clothing made from plastic—like nylon, acrylic, and polyester—presents an entirely new environmental dilemma: the garments shed in the washing machine. A 2016 study from Plymouth University found that one load of clothes can shed up to 700,000 micro-plastic particles into our waterways.

So, there's a reason *recycle* is last on the list "Reduce, Reuse, Recycle." Recycling will not save us. It should not be our first line of defense, but rather a last resort. I'm not telling you this to prevent you from recycling, though. I'm telling you this so you can learn to recycle better and depend on it less.

What Are Reducing and Reusing?

Americans buy a lot of unnecessary stuff that we don't really need. We go shopping because it makes us feel good to own something new. We're constantly bombarded by advertisements to "buy, buy, buy!" We as a society are prone to overspending and overindulging. Often times our purchases are unnecessary and clog up our homes. So before making any purchase, wait. Spend some time to think about whether or not you truly need it. In the following chapters, I will share simple ways to reframe purchases, examining and reducing what you "need," and most importantly, tips on how to seamlessly integrate these new practices into your life and daily routines. By reducing what we need, we're also reducing what we'll eventually throw out and how many resources we consume. All it takes is a few simple changes in habit.

This book contains 101 simple tips that focus on reducing and reusing. I've divided the chapters by topic so you can easily find the tip you need, whether it's how to live zero waste at home or work, on the road, or in a store.

What Is "Zero Waste"?

The goal of zero waste is to send nothing to a landfill. Reduce what we need, reuse as much as we can, send little as possible to be recycled, and compost what's leftover.

It's not a new idea, but rather a very old one. It hearkens back to depression-era living—the epitome of frugality, a time in which nothing was wasted. Very little was thrown away because people used what they had over and over again. It stands in stark contrast to our current disposable society where perfectly good items are landfilled "just because."

Zero waste is about redefining the system. We currently live in a linear economy where we take resources from the earth, use them for a while, and then dump them in a giant hole in the ground. The goal of zero waste is to move to a circular economy that mimics nature. Instead of discarding resources into a landfill, we create a system where all resources can be resumed fully back into the system for reuse. The goal is to completely write trash out of existence.

"Zero waste" doesn't really mean ZERO. Zero is a goal, but it's not possible in our current society. We will never achieve this goal without a massive overhaul and infrastructure change, but we can work toward it through individual action, group action, business action, and policy change.

Many people confuse zero waste with zero emissions. While zero emissions is an honorable goal, zero waste focuses on not creating trash. Of course, living zero waste inevitably contributes to a reduction in emissions, since it is often part of an overall practice of living more sustainably—a movement toward a much-needed circular economy. Living a zero-waste lifestyle is a call to action. It's using our lives as an act of rebellion against the wastefulness of linear economy, and it all starts with you.

Zero Waste, Natural Living, Minimalism, and How They All Tie Together

Zero-waste living is a framework. It's a set of ideas that can help you reduce your impact, and it encompasses several other popular frameworks, including natural living and minimalism.

Marketing and advertising have convinced us that it's better to let professionals take care of making all of our consumables, whether that be cleaning products, beauty products, or food items. But we don't need these products manufactured in a lab. We can easily learn the skills to make them for ourselves.

Nature has provided so much for us, and in order to sustain it for the future, it's important to get involved in our supply chain—to know where our stuff comes from and build the appreciation for all of the resources that go into growing our food and creating our products. Living a zero-waste lifestyle has helped me tune in to nature. It's been a beautiful way to connect with the seasons, living locally, and becoming semi-self-reliant. I grew up eating a semi-homemade diet. I ate well as a kid, but a lot of our veggies came from the frozen section or out of a can. I had very little experience cooking and preparing fresh vegetables. Living with the seasons helped me when I was learning how to cook. When I bought my produce from the farmers' market, I got to talk with the farmer—I got to meet the person behind my food! You can't do that in a grocery store. I learned how they grow their food and their favorite ways to prepare it. I always walked away with the tastiest produce and ten new ideas for how to cook it. You really can't beat the flavor when you buy something local and in season. It's even better when it comes from your own backyard!

Solutions for cleaning are easier than you'd think: a few simple ingredients like baking soda, soap, some vinegar, and good ol' fashion elbow grease will clean 99 percent of your home!

Throughout this book, I will teach you how to make cleaning supplies and delicious, healthy meals using simple DIY recipes, and I'll let you know what to look for when purchasing cleaning, beauty, and other products.

Minimalism and zero waste also share core principles. Both

are about being self-aware, cutting out excess, and finding your *enough*. It's about living with the things you know to be useful, the things that make you overwhelmingly happy, and cutting out the rest.

Minimalism is not a numbers game. It's not about cutting down your wardrobe to 10 items, owning fewer than 100 possessions, and living in 200 square feet. It's about finding the perfect balance of enough. It's learning to be content with what you have.

When you're content, when you're not influenced by what's trendy, and you're not focused on consuming more and more, you're using less resources. Minimalism and zero waste are both about living intentionally. Minimalism isn't about depriving yourself. It's liberating because you'll have the time and space to focus on what you truly love and forget the rest.

Can I, Just One Person, Really Make a Difference?

YES! Every day you make decisions that impact the planet. You get to decide if they're positive or negative. How do you get to work? How do you buy your groceries? What are you eating? What are you buying? Everything is interconnected. Every purchase you make is a vote for the kind of world you want to live in. *You don't vote only at the ballot box. You vote every day with every purchase you make.*

With just one small step at a time, you can greatly reduce your footprint. But, going zero waste isn't just great for the environment; it's great for you too! You'll notice an improvement in your quality of life. Side effects include eating better, feeling better, saving money, and not having to take out the trash!

CHAPTER ONE

CHANGE STARTS HERE: BEGINNER STEPS

"If you know the enemy and know yourself,
you need not fear the result of a
hundred battles. If you know yourself
but not the enemy, for every victory
gained you will also suffer a defeat. If
you know neither the enemy nor yourself,
you will succumb in every battle."
—SUN TZU

The same wisdom applies to trash.

1. Get to Know Your Trash

The first thing we're going to do is a waste audit. A waste audit is a tool to examine your personal waste stream. You'll sift through your trash and recycling to figure out exactly what you're throwing away. Going zero waste is an individual journey. There's no one-size-fits-all prescription. The waste audit will pinpoint your specific needs and provide you with a roadmap to achieve less waste.

To audit your waste, keep a clipboard by your trashcan and recycling bin. Write down every item inside, and add a tally mark next to recurring items. This will create a nice visual of where you're producing the most trash; then you can focus on solutions for the highest-ranking items. The best way to limit how much you throw away is simply to limit how much you buy and bring into your home (see Tip 2). Some of the most common items found in waste audits are paper towels (Tip 14) and food packaging (Tip 7).

2. Buy Less

The simplest way to reduce your emissions and trash output is to simply consume less. We have a huge disconnect with what we buy, leading us to buy a lot of stuff we don't need. We need to reframe our thinking. Before I make a purchase, I like to ask myself a series of questions: Where did this come from? Where is it going when I'm through with it? How was it made? Who made it? What are the resources that had to come together to make it? When we start viewing everything around us as a valuable resource, our perception and connection with "stuff" start to change.

Should I buy this?

Do you need it?

I *really* need it

Will you use it more than once a week?

YES!
Make sure it's well made.

no...

maybe?

NO

absolutely!

yes!

Can it serve more than one purpose?

it's a unitasker

Will it enrich your life?

no

I have something similar

it's multifunctional

Is it unique?

totally original

When you realize how much work goes into taking resources and crafting them into valuable products, you start to view the world a little differently. So before you make another non-essential purchase, really think about it. Take your time—I recommend at least 30 days. It allows the newness and excitement to wear down. You can really think about whether or not it's something you need.

3. Say No to Straws

Americans use 500 million plastic straws each and every day. The simplest thing you can do is ask for "No Straw" with your drink order. If you like drinking out of straws, there are a lot of reusable options like stainless steel, glass, silicone, and bamboo. Glass is my personal favorite because it doesn't impart any flavor on what you're drinking. Bamboo and stainless steel, I've found, can sometimes affect the flavor of your drink.

4. Use Reusable Grocery Bags

Using reusable bags at the grocery store is a total no-brainer for a zero-waste lifestyle. The hardest part is actually remembering to bring them with you.

If you tend to forget your reusable grocery bags, one option is to invest in a small bag or two that clip on your key ring. This way you'll be prepared with a bag at all times.

Before you leave the house, think through your day. What are your patterns? Do you typically hit up the grocery store on the way home from work on Tuesday? If you can find your patterns, you can be better prepared. The simple act of thinking through the day can prevent so much waste. As a bonus, it will also add peace and ease to your day.

5. Water Bottles

Fifty billion plastic water bottles are bought each year in the US. Plastic is made from oil, and plastic water bottles alone account for 17 million barrels of oil annually—the equivalent of powering 1 million cars for an entire year. It takes 22 gallons of water to produce 1 pound of plastic, which means it takes 3 liters of water to make 1 liter of bottled water. The footprint of bottled water is so high that beyond the resources it uses, it costs the consumer 1,000 times more than tap water—and 40 percent of all bottled water is actually taken from the tap.

To be clear, I am not anti-bottled water. In times of crisis, it is necessary, but most bottled water isn't used in a time of crisis. It's used out of laziness. If your water is drinkable, you should be drinking it. In the US, tap water is more regulated than bottled water. If you aren't a fan of how your tap water tastes, invest in a water filter (or turn to page 45 to make your own!). In the long run, it will save you a lot of money.

Ditch the disposable water bottle habit, and invest in a sturdy, reusable water bottle. There are a ton of options. I like stainless steel because it's sturdy. If you drop it, you don't have to worry about it breaking, and at the end of its life, it can be recycled. Stainless steel has a 100-percent recycling rate and can be turned into more stainless steel without loss of quality.

If you have trouble remembering to leave your house with a full bottle, here are some suggestions.

- Buy a couple of water bottles, fill them up with filtered water and keep them in the fridge. This way it's just easy to grab one and go.
- Make a mantra. Before I leave the house I always say, "Phone, Wallet, WATER, keys." This way I never have to worry about being thirsty and caught off guard.
- If you like to carry a small bag that doesn't fit a full water bottle, I fill up a stainless-steel flask. It works like a charm . . . although you might get a few strange looks, embrace it baby. No one changed the world by being normal.

Here's a zero-waste life hack I love! I like to carry a double-insulated water bottle. The double insulation keeps cold drinks cold and hot drinks hot. This way if I'm out and about, I can always use my water bottle for coffee. No need to keep a thermos *and* a water bottle with me. Two tasks, one bottle—drink options unlimited.

6. Coffee Cups

Coffee cups seem like innocent paper cups, but they are actually lined with plastic, making them virtually impossible to recycle. Very few recycling facilities have machinery capable of separating the plastic from the paper cup. If they do, once they're separated, the paper is recycled, but the plastic is thrown away. It takes a lot of energy for little reward.

The lids on disposable coffee cups are especially hazardous. They're plastic #6, polystyrene, a known carcinogen and not recyclable. (The most common form of plastic #6 is Styrofoam.) Sipping hot liquids through a polystyrene lid is less than ideal. If you forget your reusable coffee cup, ask for your coffee to go without its lid. It's what we in the zero-waste community like to call "going topless."

The best thing you can do if you order coffee to go is BYOC—bring your own cup, thermos, or bottle. (If you're brewing at home, check out Tip 13.) When you order, let the barista know how many ounces your cup holds. The barista can easily measure your coffee, and you won't accidentally pay for more coffee than fits in your cup. My thermos holds 12 ounces, the size of most small coffees.

If you forget your own cup, most coffee shops offer real mugs if you're staying there. All you have to do is ask. If you're in a rush, you can ask for your coffee at a drinkable temperature. This allows you to down your coffee without burning your tongue and be on your way without the trash.

The Ultimate Guide to Recycling

The zero-waste lifestyle is about recycling less *not* more. Have you heard the slogan: "Reduce, Reuse, Recycle"? Those instructions should be practiced in order. Before we get to recycle, we should first reduce and reuse. These Rs are often forgotten because they're not as easily actionable. How do you quantify reducing and reusing?

Recycling is more common because it is so actionable; it's tangible and we humans love to see physical, instant progress. We're not so keen on abstract ideas like reducing and reusing. It's also very hard for companies to market reducing and reusing. Both of those ideas cut into the bottom line. You know what doesn't cut into the bottom line and can actually increase sales? Recycling.

A study conducted by Boston University found that people would use more disposable products if they thought they could be recycled than they would if they thought they were going to the landfill. People's guilt over using disposable products is trumped by the good feelings that recycling produces.

Even though recycling is a last resort, it's still an important part of the process on our way to a circular economy. So, let's all do it a little better!

There is a lot of mystery around recycling. Each municipality accepts different items, making it difficult to figure out what is and isn't recyclable. A lot of people want to recycle properly, but it can be confusing to know where to start. This is a rough guide of what is generally considered to be recyclable. I encourage you to check with your local waste management facility or visit their website for more specific information on what they will accept.

Because a lot of our "recycling" isn't being recycled, it's time that we improve our recycling habits to reach that 1 percent goal (see page ix) and reduce the amount of recycling we have in the first place.

ALUMINUM CANS: Aluminum cans are one of the most valuable items in your bin. They're light like plastic and create fewer emissions when distributed than glass, and unlike plastic, aluminum is infinitely recyclable without any loss of quality. An aluminum can can go from the curbside bin to the store shelf in as little as 60 days. Aluminum cans are typically used for beverages, so after you've finished your drink, tap out the excess moisture, and the can is ready to be placed in your curbside bin. They don't need to be crushed.

ALUMINUM FOIL: Aluminum foil is reusable! If you have it, use it until it starts to flake and fall apart. And, don't forget about any aluminum pie tins or baking dishes. Wash any food scraps off of the foil and let it dry. Once it's dry, ball the aluminum foil up until it's at least 2 inches in diameter. If it's any smaller, it can get lost and wind up in the landfill. Common items containing aluminum foil that you might not think of include butter wrappers like Kerrygold and the inner wrappers of chocolate bars, bunnies, eggs, etc.

BOTTLE CAPS: Bottle caps from glass bottles of beer or soda can be made of steel or aluminum. You'll have to test it by using a magnet and separate the steel caps from the aluminum caps. You'll want to store steel caps inside of a steel can and aluminum caps inside of an aluminum one. Fill a can halfway with caps, and then place the lid of the can on top of the caps. Then crimp the opening of the can ensuring the caps and lid can't escape. You can now recycle this in your curbside bin.

BROWN PAPER: Brown paper is recyclable in your curbside bin. It's also compostable. Before recycling, see if there are any ways you can reuse it yourself. For some ideas check out page 140.

BUTCHER PAPER: Butcher paper or freezer paper is coated with plastic. It's neither recyclable nor compostable.

CARDBOARD BOXES: With the onslaught of online shopping, we have more cardboard boxes than ever before. These boxes are completely recyclable. You do NOT have to remove the tape and the labels (unless it's excessively taped all around the box), but you should break the boxes down. We should first reduce the number of products we consume that come in cardboard boxes. Then we should reuse the cardboard boxes as many times as possible. Only when the cardboard box can no longer be used should we recycle it.

CEREAL BOXES: They are recyclable in your curbside bin.

CUP LIDS: Cup lids are typically made of plastic #6. You might see "PS-6" or a "6" inside of a recycle sign.

Plastic #6 is not generally recyclable in the curbside bin. See plastic #6 on page 16 for more information.

ENVELOPES: If you have paper envelopes, be sure to remove the plastic windows before recycling. While these windows may not have been as big of a problem before the contamination rules were put in place, it is now incredibly important to keep the paper as clean as possible!

GLASS BOTTLES: Glass is infinitely recyclable without any loss of quality. It is recyclable in most municipalities. Unfortunately, some choose to crush the glass and use it as landfill cover.

MAGAZINES WITH GLOSSY PAGES: Magazines are recyclable. However, many artists use magazines as part of their art projects. See if you can reuse this material before recycling it. If you have newer magazines, donate them to libraries, waiting rooms, family shelters, nursing homes, etc.

METAL LIDS FROM GLASS BOTTLES: Lids on glass bottles, like pasta sauce or tahini, are often made from steel. You can unscrew those from the glass bottles and place them in the recycle bin. The lids are large enough that they aren't going to be lost. Typically those lids are lined with a very thin layer of plastic. Because of the high-temps used to recycle metal, it's burned off. (Just another reason why recycling shouldn't be the first line of defense.)

MILK AND JUICE CARTONS: Milk and juice cartons are made from paperboard and coated with plastic, typically polyethylene. Recycling of these items varies across the country.

NEWSPAPER: Newspaper is recyclable and compostable.

PAPER CUPS: Coffee cups, like milk cartons, are actually lined with plastic. They're not compostable, and they're not recyclable in most locations. In order to recycle coffee cups, waste management facilities have to have special machinery that separates the plastic lining from the paper cup. The lids are plastic #6 and not normally recyclable in most curbside bins, but the cardboard sleeve is recyclable!

PAPER NAPKINS AND TOWELS: The fibers are too short to be recycled, but they can be composted. Paper can only be recycled an average of eight times before it can't be recycled anymore. Each time the paper is recycled the fibers get shorter and shorter, so by the time it gets to napkins and paper towels they're too short.

PARCHMENT PAPER: Any paper that is stained with food or cooking oils is not recyclable, so parchment paper is usually out. However, you can reuse parchment paper several times and then ultimately compost it!

PASTA BOXES: Pasta boxes are recyclable, just remove the plastic window. If you buy from the brand

Jovial Foods, they use a cellulose window which is compostable in a backyard setting.

PHOTOGRAPHS: Photos are not recyclable.

PIZZA BOXES: Pizza boxes are a little tricky. Typically the bottoms of pizza boxes are too greasy to be recycled. So, you'll want to separate the lid and the bottom of your pizza box. The greasy bottom part of the pizza box can be composted, and the top of the pizza box can be recycled! (assuming the top is grease free).

You cannot recycle paper that has been soiled by food, liquids, or grease. One greasy pizza box bottom can ruin an entire bale of paper. It's important you pay attention to the other things you put in the recycle bin, so they don't ruin the recycled paper.

PLASTICS: Make sure to rinse any food or grease from your plastic, so it doesn't contaminate the paper in the bins. It doesn't have to be perfectly clean, but a quick rinse will go a long way.

It's important to note that the symbol for plastic is inside of a small recycle sign. This does NOT mean that the plastic is recyclable. Plastic has one of the lowest recycle rates. Only 9 percent of plastic ever created has been recovered, which is why it's best to reduce our dependence on plastic and opt for reusable items! It's generally considered that the lower the number of plastic, the higher the quality and the more likely it is to be accepted for recycling.

- **PLASTIC #1:** Polyethylene terephthalate (PETE or PET) is most commonly used for cake trays, soft drinks, and water bottles. Plastic #1 is accepted in most curbside bins.

- **PLASTIC #2:** High-density polyethylene (HDPE) is most commonly used for cleaning bottles, shampoo, and milk jugs. It is normally accepted in curbside bins.
- **PLASTIC #3:** PVC (vinyl) is used for cooking oil bottles, shower curtains, clear food packaging, and mouthwash bottles. Plastic #3 isn't normally accepted in curbside bins, but check with your waste management company.
- **PLASTIC #4:** Low-density polyethylene (LDPE) is used for bread bags, grocery bags, and plastic film. It is not recyclable in most curbside bins. If it is accepted in your curbside bin, then you need to put all of your plastic film inside of a plastic bag until it is roughly the size of a basketball and knot it at the top. If it's not accepted in your curbside bin, then you can take your clean, dry plastic film to the front of the grocery store where they usually accept plastic #4 in addition to plastic grocery bags.
- **PLASTIC #5:** Polypropylene (PP) is used for cheese containers, syrup bottles, yogurt containers, and is recyclable in most curbside bins.
- **PLASTIC #6:** Polystyrene (PS) is most commonly found as Styrofoam. It's used in takeaway cup lids, packing peanuts, Styrofoam blocks, cups, and takeaway containers. There are a few programs that take clean Styrofoam and turn it into molding, but those recycling options are few and far between.

Styrofoam isn't very valuable, and it's not recyclable in most locations.

- **PLASTIC #7:** Plastic #7 is composed of mixed plastics. It's often not recyclable.

PRINTER PAPER: It is recyclable in your curbside bin.

PRODUCE BAGS: Produce bags are either plastic #2 or #4, meaning they can be recycled at the front of the grocery store with other plastic film.

RECEIPTS: Receipts are coated with BPA and are not recyclable or compostable. If receipts are placed in the recycle bin they can contaminate the entire bale which means paper towels, paper napkins, and toilet paper made with 100 percent recycled content may end up containing BPA. Let's prevent this by throwing our receipts away!

SHREDDED PAPER: While crumpled and slightly altered paper is recyclable, shredded paper is not. The paper fibers have been shortened too much, and the small shreds can jam machinery and contaminate bales of other materials. Some waste management companies have special programs for recycled paper. They each have different rules for pick up so be sure to follow their requirements.

Shredded paper is great packing material, especially for fragile items. Beyond that, it's fabulous for compost—especially worm bins!

STEEL CANS: Ninety percent of all cans found in the supermarket are made from steel, which is recyclable.

Items such as canned tomatoes, chickpeas, or coconut milk are contained in steel cans. You don't have to remove the paper label from your steel can before recycling; when the cans are recycled, they are subjected to very, very high temperatures that burn off the labels. You need to rinse the cans before putting them in the recycle bin; if you leave food particles in the can, it can contaminate the bale.

You can test whether or not your can is made of steel by using a magnet. Steel is magnetic; aluminum is not. Recycling plants sort metals using magnets: the magnet will pick up the steel and the aluminum will be left behind.

STEEL CAN LIDS: Steel can lids are recyclable, but if you don't have a smooth edge can opener, you shouldn't throw them in the bin. Most recycling plants still use workers to help sort material. Before you put anything in the bin you should ask yourself, would I feel safe grabbing this? If the answer is no, you shouldn't put it in the bin. You have two options: you can take it to a transfer station for separate recycling or you can shove the lid down inside of the steel can and crimp the opening ensuring that the lid won't escape.

TETRA PAKS: Tetra paks are made up of six different layers: polyethylene, paperboard, polyethylene, aluminum, and then two more layers of polyethylene. All of these layers make them very difficult to recycle. However, they are recycled in a few places so check online.

WAX PAPER: Wax paper is a mixed bag. It can be coated with a vegetable wax or coated with a petroleum-based paraffin, and it can be hard to know which is which. If it's coated with a vegetable wax, it's compostable in an industrial setting. While it can break down in a backyard compost, there may be some difficulties. The petroleum-based paraffin coated paper is neither recyclable nor compostable.

IF YOU AREN'T SURE, CHECK WITH TERRACYCLE: TerraCycle recycles many products that would otherwise be headed to the landfill. If you have something tricky to recycle, like makeup packaging, contacts, or Brita filters, you can send them into TerraCycle to take back.

BUYING PRODUCTS FROM RECYCLED CONTENT: Very rarely are we able to buy everything we need without a package. It's important to support companies that use recycled content in their products. You have to ask yourself: are we actually recycling if we're not buying products made or packaged with recycled content?

CHAPTER TWO

KITCHEN AND COOKING

The kitchen is probably the most wasteful room in the house. You buy weekly groceries; you make three meals a day. There are a lot of easy swaps you can make to create less trash!

7. Grocery Shopping

A large part of the zero-waste lifestyle focuses on not just what you consume, but how you consume it. Have you ever thought about all the unnecessary packaging around everything you buy? Like, why is a cucumber or a head of cauliflower wrapped in plastic? There's a general consensus that plastic wrap makes food "clean." Plastic keeps food from getting dirty, but food literally comes from dirt, from the ground. It is by definition *dirty*. It's not manufactured in a lab. It doesn't sprout from the soil wrapped in three layers of plastic.

If you're used to eating a diet heavy in whole foods, this section will be easy for you. If you're used to eating a lot of processed, packaged foods, it will be a little more challenging. You can get healthy, delicious, zero-waste meals on the table in thirty minutes, but it will take time to build those habits and systems. However, I believe this is one of the most rewarding changes you can make. Good, nutrient-rich foods will help you feel amazing. That's not to say all I eat is health food. This girl gets donuts to go in her own container, and gets pizza delivered . . . just remember to compost that pizza box! (See the full guide to recycling on page 10.)

What are whole foods?
Whole foods have been minimally processed. They're ingredients rather than premade food.

Where to shop for package free items?
Farmers' markets, butchers, bakers, stores with bulk options, specialty stores, and restaurants are all great places to buy package-free groceries.

8. Go to the Farmers' Market

What to bring: a sturdy tote, several cloth or mesh produce bags, one to two sturdy containers like a mason jar or metal tiffin for easily crushed items like berries, an egg carton (you can buy eggs in the carton and then bring the cartons back to the farmer to reuse), and a water bottle in case you get thirsty while you're out.

Farmers' Markets are full of fresh, local produce. The food is grown seasonally, in your area, and picked only a day or two before the market. Produce starts to lose nutrition and flavor after it's been picked, so less travel time means a better tasting and more nutritious product. Bananas are picked 3 to 4 weeks before ever making it onto the shelves. They're picked unripe and artificially ripened in a temperature-controlled room pumped full of ethylene. If you had to choose, would you rather have a 3-week-old artificially ripened fruit or something picked from the farm two days ago?

Shopping at the farmers' market also encourages seasonal eating. In the Northern Hemisphere, it's not normal to have tomatoes in the winter. When you see tomatoes during winter at the grocery store, they have most likely been flown in from Mexico. This incurs a hefty out-of-season price tag, a lot of unnecessary emissions, and the tomatoes are lacking in flavor and nutrition.

I encourage you to embrace seasonal eating. Eating with the seasons has been therapeutic; it's helped ground me and provide a deeper connection to nature. It helps to put the cycles of life into perspective. Strawberry season doesn't last forever, but they'll be back next year. Plus, you always have something to look forward to. As blueberries fade at the end of summer, you know squash is just around the corner.

Most produce at the farmers' market is free of plastic and produce stickers. If there's a stall with something you're interested in, but it comes in plastic, ask if there's a way around it. The owner of the stall will most likely accommodate your plastic-free request. Sometimes, all it takes is asking a question. Don't be afraid to speak up. At my farmers' market, there's an egg and goat cheese stall. Both take their containers back to reuse.

If you don't have a farmers' market near you, see if you can sign up for a CSA (Community Supported Agriculture share). Local farmers will drop a box of produce at your door.

$9.$ Find Your Bulk Bins

What to bring: A sturdy tote, tightly sewn cloth bags, jars, and a water bottle in case you get thirsty while you're out.

How to Find Bulk Bins

You might be surprised how many bulk bins you have when you start looking for them. If you're looking online, you can use the Bulk Locator App (zerowastehome.com/app/) or type "bulk bins" in Yelp's search bar. This will usually turn up a few local spots. Then my biggest recommendation is to get out on foot and explore new grocery stores.

Ethnic grocery stores typically have a good selection of unpackaged offerings. I have found rice, beans, spices, and tofu in bulk at Mexican or Asian markets. I typically find baking goods, pasta, and snacks at the health-food store.

How to Shop from Bulk Bins

1. Grab a container like a mason jar.
2. Weigh the empty container and make a note of the weight. You can do this with a marker or take a picture with your phone.
3. Fill the container with whatever you like!
4. Write down the PLU or Bin #.
5. Check out. The cashier will weigh your full jar, enter the bin number to pull up the price per pound or ounce, and then they'll deduct the jar's weight.

It's that easy! I don't typically use a tare weight when I shop with thin mesh bags, because they're so light they don't register. If you're going to be filling up jars, it's important to check with a cashier or someone in the customer service department to make sure the grocery store can tare your jar. The last thing you want to do is be on the hook for the weight of your jar after you've already filled it up with treats.

> **When purchasing nuts or foods containing gluten, it's important to use a fully enclosed bag to avoid cross-contamination on carts, the floor, produce, and the conveyer belt for those with severe allergies.**

What to Do Without Bulk Bins

Not everyone will have access to bulk bins. If you don't, that's fine. It's not a requirement for going zero waste. Bulk stores don't magically make all of their food in the bulk bins. It comes to them in a package too. No one is ever going to be 100 percent zero waste, so just do the best you can! If you don't have bulk bins, opt for things packaged in paper, cardboard, aluminum, or glass—try to avoid plastic. Also, don't be afraid to buy in the same way the bulk store does. The bulk store buys 25+ pound bags of rice and beans. If you foresee yourself eating all of that without it going to waste, go ahead and cut out the middleman. Buy the big bags.

All of the recipes in this book are formulated from items I've been able to find in bulk bins or items that I purchase in recyclable packaging. I try to buy as many unpackaged things as I can, but there are still several items I buy in recyclable and compostable packaging.

Things I buy in a package with compostable packaging:

- Flour
- Baking soda
- Bamboo toothbrush
- Butter (Yes! Butter wrappers are compostable!)

Things I buy in recyclable packaging:

- Wine
- Allergy medication (And, even if medication you buy doesn't come in a recyclable package, zero waste be damned. Health comes first!)
- Dressings, hot sauces, etc.
- White vinegar, hydrogen peroxide, other first-aid-kit items

10. Go to the Butcher

What to bring: A sturdy tote, a durable container for each type of meat or cheese, and a water bottle in case you get thirsty while you're out.

When shopping for meat or cheese, I go to the local butcher. Even though I eat a plant-based diet, not everyone in my family does—although they have cut back significantly.

Diet is always a tricky subject as it is very individual. I would never tell anyone what to eat, but animal agriculture is a huge player in climate change and creates a lot of waste in the upstream. Most American meals rely heavily on animal products and grains. To reduce your impact, start looking for meals that focus on plants or plant-forward cooking. Start with the veggies, and then use meat and dairy as an accent rather than the star of the meal. Participate in Meatless Mondays or Weekday Vegetarian where you eat vegetarian or plant-based Monday through Friday.

I like going to the local butcher because I know which farm the animals came from and how they were treated. I can buy from organic, grass-fed farms, which have a lower carbon footprint than factory farms because of the carbon sequestration. When I buy meat and cheese, I use Snapware. It's a glass Pyrex-style baking dish with a plastic snap-on lid. The butcher can place the container on the scale to weigh it. With the container on the scale, they press the "tare" button. Once they press that button, it will zero out the weight of the container. Then they will fill it with whatever you want. Since the weight of the container has been subtracted, you will only be charged for what's inside.

My butcher shop also has a deli counter where they offer deli sandwich meats and cheeses. There are often deli counters at regular grocery stores, and you can bring your own containers there as well.

11. Visit the Baker

What to bring: A sturdy tote, several cloth bags, a tiffin or large container for anything covered in frosting, and a water bottle in case you get thirsty while you're out.

Who doesn't love fresh bread? Most towns or neighborhoods I've lived in have a local bakery. Many grocery stores have a bakery department too. My local bakery has a great system. They have dozens of tongs hanging on a rack beside the bakery cases. Next to the tongs are stacks of colorful cafeteria trays. You use the tongs to pick out your goodies and place them on the tray. Once your tray is full, you head to the register. They'll offer to brown bag it, or you can place the goodies in your own containers.

I pack a cloth bag full of rolls and a large tin full of cinnamon rolls or donuts. I place frosted items into a sturdy container, to avoid washing frosting out of my cloth bags. My shop offers a 10-cent discount if you bring your own container. The shop owner saves money, you save money, and you prevent unnecessary waste.

In order to keep bread fresh, I store a small portion that we'll eat in two days inside a ceramic bread box. I store the rest of the bread in a cloth bag in the freezer. The rolls will stay as fresh as the day I bought them for up to a month—after 4 to 5 weeks they start to develop freezer burn.

12. Specialty Stores and Restaurants

What to bring: A sturdy tote, original containers, appropriate containers to match what you're getting, and a water bottle in case you get thirsty while you're out.

A lot of specialty stores offer refill programs. You'll find these stores among cute downtown shops, malls, strip malls, and touristy areas. Most are off the beaten path and will take some time to find. In my experience, the owners of these small businesses have been exceedingly helpful, but don't have a strong web presence.

Things I buy from specialty stores:

- Spices
- Olive oil
- Vinegar
- Wine
- Beer

In most of these stores, you purchase the goods in their container. After you've finished the product, clean the container, bring it back for a refill, and you'll receive a discount. Once you find these places, their high-quality product and customer service will keep you coming back.

In my experience, the olive oil, vinegar, and spices have been superior quality to what's in the grocery store, and cheaper, too. Beer and wine have been better quality but more expensive.

Either way, I feel really good about supporting a local business in my community.

If you have a local brewery, check to see if they offer growler refills. Some wineries and wine bars have refill events where you can fill any 750 ml bottle, and the wine bar I go to has branded swing-top bottles for the special red blend they keep on tap.

Restaurants are another place to find specialty items. Just because something's from a restaurant, don't assume it's more expensive. On average, I've found that buying things there costs the same or less than buying from the grocery store, and the quality is better because products are made daily as opposed to sitting around on a shelf.

I buy tortillas, tortilla chips, and sometimes salsa from a local Mexican restaurant or the local tortilleria. I buy my pizza dough from the local pizza parlor. I walk in and ask for these items to go in my own container, and I have never been turned down thus far.

COST COMPARISON

Item	Restaurant	Grocery Store
25 (8-inch) tortillas	$2.00	$6.00
1 bag tortilla chips	$2.50	$3.50
Pizza dough for 1 large pizza	$3.00	$3.00

13. Coffee and Tea

Got a morning caffeine addiction?

Keurig and other pod machines produce an inferior cup of coffee for a superior price, and they amass a ton of plastic waste. Even though Nespresso offers recyclable pods, that's not an overall solution since their pods are only recyclable through a store program (not curbside). Remember, zero waste isn't about recycling more; it's about recycling less.

Also, the individual pods aren't great for your health or the health of the planet. Imagine all of that hot water running through a plastic #7 K-cup that's not recyclable and not guaranteed to be free of endocrine disruptors.

If you love your pod machine, you can buy refillable K-cups and fill them with coffee grounds. As a bonus, it's much cheaper to buy coffee grounds than it is to buy pods.

> Endocrine disruptors interfere with our hormones. They can cause certain hormones to overproduce or underproduce and disrupt our body's natural communication system. You can learn more about the endocrine system in Tip 24.

Drip Coffee: Drip-coffee pots have been a staple for many years. The drip-coffee machines I've seen come with a washable filter, so you don't have to use a paper filter. If you need to use a filter with your drip-coffee pot, you can buy a reusable one or unbleached paper filters that can be composted with the coffee grounds inside.

Espresso Machine: The espresso machines I've used produce a single cup of coffee like a Keurig but without the waste of a pod. Some even grind the coffee beans and brew all in the same machine. With a wand for steaming milk, you can make a lot of lattes without the coffee shop price tag.

The only waste in this setup is running a descaling agent through the machine. You can buy a liquid descaling agent that comes in a plastic bottle that can be recycled. While recycling isn't ideal, it's still much better to maintain the things you own. Keeping the machine descaled, clean, and in good repair is a huge part of living a zero-waste lifestyle. It reduces waste in the long run because you're using resources already in the waste stream for as long as possible and you're driving down the demand for new resources.

High-quality espresso machines are built to last and designed for repairs and maintenance. When making a new purchase, look for items designed to be repaired. Unfortunately, Keurigs were not designed to be repaired. They're intentionally built to be difficult or more expensive to repair so when it breaks you have to buy a new one. It's an example of what is called *planned obsolescence*. It's how companies force you to buy new products to increase their sales. It's one of the many flaws of a linear economy.

Pour Over: Pour-over coffee makers use glass or ceramic carafes. With these, you use either a stainless-steel filter or a reusable cloth coffee filter. You place your coffee in the filter and pour hot water over the grounds very slowly. It's a tasty and totally zero-waste way of making coffee.

French Press: This is how I brew my coffee and loose leaf tea. My French press has a glass base, stainless frame, and a stainless plunger. I scoop two heaping tablespoons of coffee grounds into the base, and then I pour in a cup of very hot water. I let the grounds steep for four minutes, and then I plunge down the grounds, trapping them while I pour out a delicious cup of coffee. When I'm finished, I either compost my grounds or turn them into a body scrub.

> **Before you compost your grounds, you can use them to create a rejuvenating body scrub! Check out Tip 45.**

Tea: Most tea bags actually contain plastic these days. Yep, you're steeping your tea with a side of polypropylene. Instead, opt for loose leaf tea with a tea strainer or use a French press!

14. Paper Towels

Swap out paper towels for tea towels or dishcloths. You'll want to opt for cotton towels with a large open weave. An open weave helps to absorb water instead of just pushing it around.

Once the cotton towels get too ratty, you can demote them to really dirty jobs. Then at the end of their lives, you can compost them. I don't recommend microfiber towels because they're plastic and like all plastic textiles (including polyester, acrylic, spandex, rayon, and nylon) they shed micro-plastic particles into the waterways when washed. Opt for natural fibers instead. If you really love your microfiber towels, look at buying a Guppy Bag, which catches micro-plastic pieces. The best thing you can do is to wash the rags less, and then choose a natural fiber alternative when the time comes to replace your supply.

After-Meal Clean-up: Don't reach for a paper towel. Brush all the crumbs into the sink or the palm of your hand. If your mess is sticky, dampen the cloth towel and wipe it up.

Windows and Glass: You don't need paper towels to get a streak-free shine. The secret is to continually wipe the window or mirror until it's dry and the streaks will disappear. I also hear that newspaper works well in a pinch!

Grease: When there's grease left in the pan, depending on how much there is, I'll either sauté with it or store it in a mason jar for later. If there's not enough for either of those things, I leave it to season the skillet or take a piece of bread and use it to absorb the grease. Cut the bread into chunks to make croutons or compost it in an industrial composting facility.

If you like to pat the grease dry on something like bacon, here's an alternative: place the cooked bacon on a cooling rack and put a plate or baking sheet underneath to catch the grease.

Drying Produce or Meat: After you wash your produce, dry it with a cloth towel instead of a paper one. Meat is a trickier subject. Oftentimes you'll hear chefs say to pat your meat dry before cooking. Instead of patting it dry, I put it naked on a cooling rack on top of a baking sheet in the fridge for at least a couple of hours, but preferably overnight. This dries the meat, resulting in crispy skin and no worries about paper towels.

The Gross Stuff: I wipe up vomit, mud, or gross smashed food with a cloth towel and rinse it off in the sink. Then, I hand wash the towel and hang it to dry. I do understand, though, the desire to keep a spare roll of paper towels around for this reason. Just make sure to compost the paper towels when you're done and try to use them sparingly.

15. Aluminum Foil

After spending some time away from aluminum foil, I realized I really didn't need it.

Lining Pans: Instead of lining pans with aluminum foil, I use the pans themselves. They wash clean fairly easily, and if not, I use a bamboo pot scraper which always does the job in a matter of seconds. If you prefer lining your pans, check out silicone baking mats. They're very versatile in the kitchen; I use my silicone mats for freezing way more than baking.

Preventing Burning when Baking: When baking a pie or turkey for Thanksgiving, I used to always put aluminum foil on certain areas to keep them from browning too much. But they actually make pie rings to keep the crust from burning, and to cover the turkey I've found I can just set a 9-inch cake tin on top to cover the breast. It's a perfect fit!

Wrapping Food for Storage: Occasionally, I'd wrap odd shaped foods like a piece of pie or a piece of pizza with aluminum foil. The foil did well conforming to the shape, and then I'd store it in the fridge. Now, I wrap odd-shaped food in beeswax wraps or place it in Snapware. (See the box on page 48 for an introduction to Snapware, my favorite glassware replacement for plastic Tupperware containers.)

16. Plastic Wrap

I've never been a big fan of plastic wrap, and I never found much use for it in the home.

Waiting for Dough to Rise: One of the most common uses I've seen is waiting for dough to rise. Instead of wrapping the bowl with plastic wrap simply throw a tea towel over the bowl.

Sealing Food for Later: If you have leftovers, I've seen people wrap the bowl or plate with plastic wrap to save for later.

- If you have a bowl, you can set a plate on top.
- You can also wrap the plate with a beeswax wrap.
- You can also transfer the food into a mason jar or Tupperware-style container. (See Tip 20—I always use glass Snapware, since glass is safer than plastic.)

Carrying Food to a Party: Instead of wrapping a bowl with plastic wrap, look for mixing bowls or party dishes with removable lids.

How to Make a Beeswax Wrap

Use a cotton fabric with the thickness and tightness of a bedsheet. Old bedsheets or pillow cases work great! Cut into desired shapes: 14" x 14" squares will cover bowls and sandwiches or opt for 24" x 17" for loaves of bread.

Melt a small bowl of beeswax using a double boiler. Once melted pour a small amount onto the cotton cloth. Use a brush or silicone spatula to evenly distribute the beeswax on both sides of the fabric.

Let the fabric dry by hanging it on a clothesline leaving both sides fully exposed to the air. Once it's dry, it's ready to use! Don't wash the beeswax wraps in the dishwasher or use really hot water. They might melt.

When washing your brush, spatula, bowl, or anything else you used with the melted beeswax, rinse it with boiling water! Beeswax is notoriously difficult to clean. Just *bee* careful so you don't burn yourself.

17. How to Store Food Without Plastic to Keep It Fresh as Long as Possible

In the US, we waste 40 percent of our food. With that food, we could feed 60 million people a year, but instead, we're tossing it into the landfill. Organic matter makes up 60 percent of the waste in landfills and is responsible for 16 percent of all methane emissions in the US.

If that's not enough to make you think about what you're buying at the grocery store, the average American household throws out $2,275 worth of food every year. Here are two things you can do to avoid food waste:

- Before you go to the store make sure you make a note of the food you already have and plan meals around the older food. We'll go further in depth on meal planning in Tip 25.
- Make sure you're storing your produce for optimal freshness.

Guide to Storing Produce
Store in a cool, dark, dry spot
Bananas: Disassemble the bunch and store as single bananas
Garlic
Onions: Keep away from potatoes
Potatoes and sweet potatoes: Keep away from onions
Shallots

Ripen at room temperature, then move to the fridge. This type of produce doesn't need to be stored any special way. It can sit on a shelf or in the crisper drawer.

Apricots

Avocados

Guava

Kiwifruit

Mangos

Melons

Nectarines

Papayas

Passion fruit

Peaches

Pears

Persimmons

Pineapple

Plantains

Plums

Tomatoes

Keep in the refrigerator

Artichokes: Spritz with water and store in a bowl

Asparagus: Place the stalks in a cup of water

Beets: Remove the greens, chop, and place in an airtight container like a mason jar. Use the greens like spinach and wash right before using. Store the beets loose.

Berries: Store in an airtight mason jar

Bell Peppers: Chop into sticks or dice, store them in an airtight mason jar. Or store them loose and whole.

Broccoli: Loose in the crisper drawer

Brussel Sprouts: Store in an airtight mason jar

Cabbage: Loose in the crisper drawer

Carrots: Store submerged in a glass of water. Swap the water every 2 to 3 days.

Cauliflower: Loose in the crisper drawer

Celery: Wrap in a tea towel and keep in the crisper

Cherries: Store in an airtight mason jar

Corn: Store loose in the crisper drawer with the husk on

Cranberries

Cucumber: Loose in the crisper drawer or pre-slice and store in an airtight mason jar

Eggplant: Loose in the crisper drawer

Figs: Wrap in a tea towel

Grapes: Store in a bowl on a shelf

Green Beans: Loose in the crisper drawer

Green Onions: Store the roots in a cup of water

Kale: Chop and place in an airtight container like a mason jar or large mixing bowl with a lid. Wash right before eating.

Leeks: Loose in the crisper drawer

Lettuce: Chop and place in an airtight container like a mason jar or large mixing bowl with a lid. Wash right before eating.

Mushrooms: Store open in a bowl on a shelf

Peas: Store in an airtight mason jar

Radishes: Remove the greens, chop, and place in an airtight container like a mason jar. Use the greens with other salad greens and wash right before using. Store the radishes loose.

Rhubarb: Wrap in a tea towel

Spinach: Chop and place in an airtight container like a mason jar or large mixing bowl with a lid. Wash right before eating.

Turnips: Chop and keep in an airtight mason jar

Zucchini: Loose in the crisper drawer

Don't wash produce until you're about to eat it!
Especially berries.

○

Store greens with a cloth napkin to absorb
unwanted moisture

○

Eat food prone to spoilage first and save heartier
produce for later in the week

18. Filter Water

Depending on where you live, your tap water might not taste the best. Thankfully, there's an easy way to filter water that doesn't rely on plastic. Of course, if you already have a plastic filter, use it until you can't use it anymore.

The main ingredient inside filter cartridges is activated carbon, which is the same thing as activated charcoal, and you can buy activated charcoal sticks. Activated charcoal sticks are exactly what they sound like. They're sticks, and they've had all their moisture removed, making them very porous. I use Kishu sticks because they come wrapped in paper.

Activated charcoal naturally bonds with toxins, allowing the porous surface to trap the toxins inside. The sticks remove mercury, chlorine, copper, and even lead, but they don't remove fluoride. The fluoride molecule is very small, and it's difficult for the charcoal to bond with. Every month, you should boil the charcoal sticks in a pot of water to release the toxins. Depending on frequency of use, the sticks will last four to six months.

I store my water in an old glass milk jug and place the charcoal stick inside. You can use any sort of glass carafe with a lid. Fill your carafe with tap water, place the stick inside, and in 1 to 2 hours you'll have filtered water. I keep the stick in the water, and I don't remove it to make life easier. I also like to keep two jugs in the fridge so while one is filtering, I can have fresh water on hand in the other.

If you're looking for a solution to remove fluoride, the Berkey filter will do the job. The Berkey filter is a two-part stainless tankard. They take up a little bit more space, but they do a great job of filtering water!

19. Plastic Baggies

When I was in school, I had a peanut butter and jelly sandwich for lunch every day. Each sandwich came wrapped in an individual plastic baggie, and I threw away every single one. I sent approximately 2,275 sandwich bags sent to the landfill.

I still love sandwiches and pack them for my work lunches, but I wrap them in a cloth napkin, a beeswax wrap, or I place them in a metal tiffin. If you need something a little more heavy duty or if you prep freezer meals, you can buy reusable silicone bags called Stasher Bags. They make a number of sizes from snack size to gallon size. You can wash them in the dishwasher, and they are infinitely reusable. Silicone is a very sturdy material, and if for any reason yours stops working you can send it back to the company where they turn it into playground pebbles.

20. What about My Plastic Tupperware?

Plastic is toxic, and it can leach toxins into your food. When storing food, I opt for glass containers like Snapware, silicone bags, beeswax wraps, and stainless-steel tiffins. For a complete guide to plastic-free storage for produce, check out Tip 17.

Throwing your old plastic Tupperware away and getting brand new eco-friendly items would be contrary to the zero-waste lifestyle. If you want to ditch plastic around your food for health reasons, you can demote your old plastic instead of throwing it out. Here are a few ideas to use it around your home. (We'll talk more about removing toxic items from your home in Tip 24.)

For Compost

I use large plastic Tupperware containers as compost buckets in my freezer both at home and at work. It makes it easy to transport the compost from the work freezer home or to transport my compost from the freezer to the outside bin.

At Work

I brought several Tupperware containers to work. I use them to organize odds and ends in my desk drawers, and I keep some in the work kitchen. They are handy for office leftovers, like when a client brings in a tray of goodies that need to be stored in the fridge.

Storage

We use several of our old Tupperware containers in the garage where they hold all sorts of things like screws, nails, etc. They can be used in the bathroom to hold bobby pins and hair ties. I even have two that hold jewelry in the bedroom.

Don't forget about the junk drawer too. Yes, I still have a junk drawer to hold important do-dads like batteries, wires, and miscellaneous office supplies. I use a small container to hold expired batteries, so I can take them down to the battery recycling box at Best Buy.

My favorite Tupperware-style container is actually a glass version called Snapware. It's glass on the bottom with a leak-proof plastic lid that locks into place. If you hand wash the lids, they will last a long time. I like that the Snapware is clear so you can easily see what needs to be eaten in the fridge. Storing leftover food in glass containers helps to avoid food waste.

21. Real Plates, Real Flatware

Opt for real plates and real flatware instead of paper plates and plastic cutlery. People often use paper plates to try and save water, but it's important to look at the waste and resource upstream when making decisions. Did you know it takes 8 gallons of water to make one paper plate? Choosing to use real plates and real flatware is a simple way to cut down on your resource consumption.

22. Cloth Napkins

Cloth napkins are a nice addition to the dinner table. We used to only break the cloth napkins out for holidays and special occasions, but now I honestly can't imagine eating without them.

The switch to cloth napkins is pretty simple; once you're in a routine, it's second nature. I keep a large basket of cloth napkins on the table. At mealtime, we grab a napkin from the basket. After dinner, if the napkin is clean, it stays at that person's place setting. If that napkin is dirty, it goes into the hamper or it goes directly into the washing machine, so it's automatically washed with the next load.

Washing cloth napkins takes a very small amount of room in your loads. You won't notice any difference in your water bill.

23. Compostable Dish Scrubs

It's best to try and avoid disposable items, but sometimes you really don't have a choice. I don't know of any dish brush that lasts forever so the best solution is to go for ones that are compostable. The tools I can't live without are a bamboo pot scraper, a bamboo bottle brush, and a bamboo pot brush. Bamboo scrubbies are more sanitary and last a lot longer than sponges. The average bamboo brush lasts one to two years, and as a bonus, they're more aesthetically pleasing than their plastic counterparts.

24. Swapping Out Toxic Items

I'm always hesitant to recommend anyone throw anything out. I feel like tossing items for the sake of upgrading to new "fancy, eco-friendly" items is inherently un-eco-friendly.

I don't believe there's anything wrong with purchasing an item that will bring you joy and make your life easier, but you should be wary of how you choose to spend your dollars and refer back to Tip 1. Really examine the seller's message. Are they just trying to sell you something? Does their company give back? Do they go into explicit detail of where their products are sourced and manufactured? If a company is trying to have a positive impact, they'll be honest and upfront. They'll want to tell you about the good things they're doing, and they will be able to speak about it in highly specific terms.

The only time I recommend throwing away your belongings is if they're toxic.

I approached zero waste through a health lens: Many everyday items like cleaning products, beauty products, furniture with flame-retardants, Teflon pots, dental floss coated with PFCs, and plastic contain endocrine disruptors. Now, lots of things can disrupt the endocrine system: really simple stuff like stress, lack of sleep, and too much sugar and caffeine (the four pillars of college). But, the endocrine system can also be disrupted by xenoestrogens—synthetic or natural chemical compounds that mimic estrogen. Estrogen is responsible for tissue growth and development specifically for breasts, skin, and the reproductive system. Too much estrogen (or exposure to xenoestrogens) can cause unnatural growths like tumors and cysts. It can also cause weight gain and throw off the balance of the entire endocrine system, which affects our ability to regulate hormones. I had a breast cancer scare when I was 20, and now I'm very cautious of the products I bring into my home. My hormones don't need any more stress, so I try to avoid unnecessary contact. Living in today's world it's impossible to remove all contact, but by phasing out toxic products and reducing my exposure to plastic I can significantly reduce my exposure and symptoms like pain, breakouts, bloating, and exhaustion.

In the kitchen, this means no plastic Tupperware around my food, avoiding purchasing food in plastic, not using plastic cutting boards, and not using Teflon pans.

If you use Teflon pans or plastic cutting boards, I would recommend that you phase those out for safer alternatives. I use wooden cutting boards, cast-iron pans, and ceramic-coated pots. While these are a bigger investment, they last forever! I have two pans (an 8" and 12" skillet) and two pots (a small 2-quart saucepan and a 5-quart Dutch oven). I love cooking and I've never needed any more than four pots/pans—after all, my stove only has four burners.

25. Meal Planning and Prepping

Meal planning is the key to eating healthy *and* preventing food waste. And it can be simple, I promise. I've come up with a foolproof way to meal plan that allows for flexibility. You aren't going to be locked into eating lasagna on Tuesday night if you don't want lasagna on Tuesday night.

The first step is to make a list of all of your favorite meals. Compile this list with your family. Write down everyone's favorite meals. You need at least 20, but 40 is ideal. As an example, here are a few of our favorite family meals:

Lentil shepherd's pie	Spaghetti
Veggie burgers	Chicken/eggplant parmesan
Pizza	Lasagna
Potpie	Fried rice
Mac & cheese	Beef/mushroom and broccoli
Quesadillas	Cheesesteak/mushroom subs
Fajitas	Sloppy joes
Nachos	Caesar salad

Pro Tip: **Install a list app on your phone. It doesn't have to be fancy, just one where you can easily check and uncheck which meals you can make from the groceries you have in your pantry.**

Once you have a full list, organize it by flavor profile. For example, the list above has American, Italian, Mexican, and Asian flavors, and within each group, most of the recipes call for the same ingredients.

You might not know ahead of time what you'll be craving on Tuesday, but you should be able to figure out the frequency of your cravings. I *know* I want pizza at least once a week. I also know that I want Mexican food every day. Based on cravings I can map out a week's worth of meals, such as two American dinners, two Mexican dinners, pizza, one dinner out, and leftovers or Asian food at some point during the week. When you're shopping based on flavor profile, you can keep your spices and base ingredients stocked in the pantry. Since I know I'll be making at least two American dinners I make sure I'm stocked up on the ingredients I need for my favorite American meals, such as potatoes, lentils, chickpeas, butter, and flour. Then I buy a couple of in-season vegetables. So, if I want to make a potpie in the winter, it may have butternut squash and carrots. If I want to make a potpie in the spring, I'll use carrots and peas.

If I'm shopping for Mexican food, I make sure I have tortillas, tortilla chips, pinto beans, and salsa on hand. In the summer I use plenty of peppers and corn. In the winter I use heartier produce like sweet potatoes and cauliflower.

When you shop based on flavor profile, you have the freedom to eat what you want on any given day of the week and have complete flexibility with ingredients.

Utilizing your freezer to prevent food waste: It's helpful to have a stocked pantry and freezer for quick, easy meals. We freeze cooked beans and produce if it looks like it's going to turn before we can eat it. It's also a great way to keep produce past its season without canning. I still have three jars of peas! Wash and cut your produce. Place it on a flat baking sheet to freeze. This will prevent the pieces from clumping together, and you can pull out exactly how much you need for a recipe. Once your produce has frozen all the way through, transfer it to a container.

Another easy way to prevent food waste is to understand the difference between Use-By, Best-By, and Sell-By Dates.

Use-By: The product should be eaten by this day. At this point, the food quality will start to go down, but it doesn't mean the item will make you sick. These dates are not an exact science. Products can go bad before or after these dates. The most reliable way to tell is with a smell and taste test.

Best-By: This is the date by which the product should be eaten for optimum quality, but it doesn't mean the product has gone bad.

Sell-By: This label is for retailers. It lets the store know when the product should be sold. It doesn't have anything to do with whether or not the food is safe to consume.

26. Recipes for Cooking with Scraps

Before you take your food to the compost bin, ask yourself, "Could I eat that?" A lot of resources go into growing our food, and we should treat it with respect by doing our best to eat all of it. There are so many delicious meals you can make with food scraps, but here are a few of my favorite recipes.

BROCCOLI STEM SLAW
I like to serve this slaw on top of pulled jackfruit BBQ sandwiches or in tacos with black beans.

1 cup peeled and julienned broccoli stem (about 1 medium broccoli stem)
1 cup julienned carrots
1 cup julienned green apples
1 cup julienned red peppers
2 cloves garlic, minced
2 tablespoons olive oil
2 tablespoons soy sauce or tamari
1 tablespoon rice vinegar
½ teaspoon sesame oil
Juice of ½ lime

Toss all of the ingredients in a mixing bowl.

CARROT TOP PESTO

Toss this pesto with pasta or use it as a dip for carrot sticks. I also like to add this spread on a delicious summer tomato sandwich.

  1 cup chopped carrot greens (use the leafy parts not the
      stalks)
  ¼ cup pistachios
  Juice of 1 lemon
  2 garlic cloves
  2 tablespoons nutritional yeast
  ¼ cup olive oil
  ½ cup water
  Salt and pepper to taste

Add all ingredients to a blender and blend for 1 minute until creamy.

STRAWBERRY TOP TEQUILA

When you eat strawberries, save the fruit that you cut off with these leaves to make this strawberry-infused tequila. I like to use it in summer cocktails like strawberry margaritas.

  12 strawberry tops
  1 cup tequila

Add the ingredients to a mason jar and screw on the lid. Let it sit for 2 to 3 days. Remove the tops before using.

SCRAP STOCK

Keep veggie scraps like the end of celery, carrot ends, carrot peels, onion peels, garlic peels, mushroom stems, green onions stems, leek tops, and leftover herbs like thyme or parsley. I don't recommend adding kale stems or broccoli stems as they might make the stock bitter.

1. Add the scraps and two bay leaves to a slow cooker.
2. Add enough water to cover the scraps.
3. Cook on high for four hours or low for eight hours.
4. Use the stock to make rice, quinoa, soup, or stuffing. Freeze the leftover stock in mason jars.

How to freeze in mason jars: fill 2 inches below the lid in wide-mouth jars. If you have a small-mouth jar, fill 2 inches below the shoulder. (The stock will expand as it freezes, so if you don't leave this space, the jar might crack.)

27. Composting

Composting is awesome. It completes the circle of life. You eat an apple all the way to the core. When you're done, you place the core in your compost pile, and after a while, it becomes a nutrient-rich soil that you can use to grow more apples—how cool is that!

The average US household produces 650 pounds of organic trash a year, but most of that is landfilled. In fact, 60 percent of our landfills are full of organic matter. You think it would break down since it's dumped into a giant hole in the ground, but it doesn't because landfills aren't aerated. Organic and inorganic materials are mixed, so instead of the organic matter decomposing, it's preserved along with the inorganic material forever. It's called anaerobic decomposition, and all of that oxygen-deprived organic matter releases methane into the atmosphere. Methane is 30 percent more powerful than CO_2.

Thankfully, composting is pretty easy. You can do it in your backyard, in your house, through a municipal program, a community garden, or even use a business service. Some of you may have access to an industrial compost program offered through your city or a third party. It's definitely worth a quick Google search. Having someone else handle your compost makes it a no-brainer. Whether it's through the city or a third party, they will drop off a bucket or bin. You fill the bin with organic matter, and when it's full, they'll pick it up and turn it into nutrient-rich compost. Depending on the service, you might have to pay a small fee.

BUSTING THE MYTH!

Compost does not smell bad. The reason your trash stinks is because organic and non-organic materials are mixed. Just like in the landfill, the organic matter can't break down, so it lets off really stinky odors. When the organic matter is surrounded by other organic matter, like dirt, it can break down and won't let off stinky smells.

What Can You Actually Compost?

You can compost any organic material:

Ashes

Bones*

Cereal boxes

Cobs

Coffee grounds

Dairy*

Dryer lint (if most of your clothes are made from natural fibers)

Egg cartons (not Styrofoam or plastic ones!)

Eggshells

Fish*

Flowers

Fruit and veggie peels

Grass clippings

Hair

Hay or straw

Herbivore manure

Leaves

Meat*

Natural fibers in small pieces: wool, cotton, linen, hemp, silk

Newspaper

Non-plastic tea bags

Nutshells

Paper bags

* Can only be composted in an industrial facility

Pizza boxes

Sawdust

Shredded paper

Stalks

Tea

Toilet paper cores

Unbleached organic cotton
tampons

Unbleached paper towels
and napkins

Vacuum dust

What Type of Bin Is Right for You?

- An enclosed bin requires very little maintenance. You throw your food scraps in, stir it with a shovel, and water it occasionally, but all in all, it's pretty hands off. They have lids to keep out critters, and they're aerated with small holes along the tops and sides. At the bottom, they have a small door that can be opened to take out the fully developed compost, while you keep adding new scraps to the top. This method takes the longest to turn the scraps into soil. You can buy these, or there are a lot of DIY projects that show you how to make your own.

- A tumble compost bin is also very low maintenance. Throw in your food scraps and turn the bin every so often to get proper aeration. These tumblers come with either one or two compartments. If there's only one, you have to wait until the entire tumbler has composted before you can add any new material. It should only take a month to turn your trash into soil.

- Trench compost: You can always dig a hole! Go into your backyard dig a hole 6" deep, place your scraps in the hole, and cover. The scraps should decompose in about a month.

- If you're in an apartment without a yard, don't fear. You still have a ton of options. Worm bins are conducive to apartment living. You can make your own bin, or you can buy one, and fill it with red wigglers. Red wigglers can be found at your local bait shop. For happy worms, keep the soil moist, not wet, with a spray bottle full of water, and have an adequate mix of browns (paper) and greens (food scraps). The worms are temperature sensitive, and it's best to keep them indoors. Unfortunately, you cannot compost citrus, but you can always turn your citrus peels into a delicious candied treat—eat those scraps!

If you're not interested in the DIY composting route and you don't have a city or third-party program, you still have a couple of options:

- See if you know someone who composts and would take your scraps
- See if any neighbors have chickens. They usually eat almost all of our typical food scraps.
- Check with farmers at your farmers' market. They often will use it to grow more food.
- Check with your local community garden

CHAPTER THREE

BATHROOM PRODUCTS AND PERSONAL CARE

The bathroom, although a small room, can create some serious trash. A lot of people forget to sort their bathroom trash and throw away perfectly recyclable items like toilet paper cores. Stack the most common disposable items like Q-tips, tampons, pads, and cotton rounds—you've got a few simple changes that can add up to a massive impact.

28. Dental Floss

Most floss doesn't just come in plastic—it *is* plastic. Beyond being plastic, it's coated with perfluorochemicals also known as PFCs which are added to make the floss glide better. PFCs are also found in Teflon and have been linked to thyroid disease, dementia, cancer, fertility issues, and birth defects. PFCs can be left behind after flossing and are easily absorbed into the body. It's best to look for safer alternatives. I use silk floss from Dental Lace that can be composted. As a bonus, the dental lace comes in a refillable glass jar with a metal lid.

I also use a water flosser, which uses a powerful jet stream of water to stimulate and improve gum health; they're especially great if you have dental hardware.

29. Toothpaste

Oral health is so important, and there's no one-size-fits-all solution. I use a homemade tooth powder, and my husband uses toothpaste. We both go to the dentist every six months for routine cleanings to make sure we're doing what's best for our health.

The DIY option might work great for you or it might not, but there's no reason creating waste should ever stop you from doing what's best for your health. We don't live in a perfect zero-waste world and trash is going to happen—always put your health first.

If you continue to buy toothpaste, be sure to watch out for microbeads! They're small plastic beads that are too small to be filtered, so they're released into our waterways and oceans. Plastic acts as a sponge and can absorb bacteria. Fish often mistake microbeads for food, poisoning themselves and the food chain.

DIY

My grandmother, who used toothpowder growing up, helped me with my recipe. After we worked on the recipe, I contacted a dentist to see what they had to say. The dentist recommended plain baking soda. Baking soda is less abrasive than most commercial toothpaste, but my teeth are a little sensitive. The baking soda was a little too harsh, and this was the recipe we wound up with.

I'm really fortunate that I can find all of these ingredients in bulk at my local health food store. They aren't located with the food, but they're located in the beauty section. If you can't find these items in bulk, reference Tip 9.

EVERYDAY TOOTH POWDER

- 1 part xylitol: It's a natural sweetener. It prevents bacteria from sticking to the teeth and neutralizes the pH to help avoid tooth decay.
- 1 part baking soda: A very mild abrasive that dislodges plaque on teeth, breaks down stain-causing molecules, and neutralizes pH.
- 1 part bentonite clay: Draws out toxins, contains calcium, and is often used to help remineralize teeth. (Avoid using metal utensils with the clay; metal can deactivate it.)

Mix the powder together with a wooden spoon and store in a small glass jar. To apply the toothpowder, dampen your toothbrush, shake off any excess water, and gently dip into the powder.

WHITENING TOOTH POWDER

I don't recommend using this tooth powder every day; 2 to 3 times a week is fine, but stop if you notice any sensitivity.

- 1 part xylitol
- 1 part baking soda
- 1 part bentonite clay
- 1 part activated charcoal

Mix all of the ingredients together and store in a small glass jar. (Remember to avoid using a metal utensil.)

Fluoride Treatments: I have fluoridated tap water, so I'm not too concerned about my toothpowder lacking fluoride, but if you really benefit from fluoride you can get a fluoride treatment at the dentist with your regular cleanings.

Metal Tubes and Toothy Tabs: If you're not a fan of the DIY, there are several companies who sell toothpaste in metal tubes much like the original toothpaste tubes sold in the late 1800s. They come with a crank so you can squeeze out every last drop. Metal tubes are recyclable, unlike their plastic counterparts. Cut the bottom off the tube to get out every last drop of toothpaste and then clean the tube before recycling.

Toothy Tabs are relatively new, but they're small and look like pills. You pop one tab in your mouth, bite down, and then brush. They come in glass jars or cardboard boxes.

Take-Back Programs: If you benefit from fluoride in your toothpaste, several toothpaste companies have partnered with TerraCycle to take back empty tubes.

30. Toothbrush

Every plastic toothbrush ever created still exists. Yes, all of the toothbrushes you've used are still out there, but it doesn't have to be that way. A toothbrush is a great first zero-waste swap. Instead of using a plastic toothbrush, opt for a toothbrush made from bamboo!

The only fully compostable toothbrush on the market uses pig hair for bristles. It was how they made all toothbrushes up until the '40s. Using pig hair to brush my teeth kind of freaks me out, so I use a toothbrush made by Brush with Bamboo. They're pioneering the way with their bristles and working toward a fully compostable plant-based product. Right now, they're using 62 percent plant-based materials and 38 percent plastic.

In order to properly dispose of your bamboo toothbrush, you'll need to remove the bristles, which can easily be done with a pair of pliers. The bamboo stick can be composted or used for kindling in the fire, but before you even get to the composting stage, hold on to your toothbrushes! They work great for small cleaning jobs.

31. Cotton Swabs

You might not even need cotton swabs. They should never go inside the ear. They're only supposed to clean the outer part of the ear, which can easily be done with a washcloth.

Most cotton swabs have a plastic base connecting both of the cotton ball ends. This makes them unrecyclable. If you need cotton swabs, opt for the sticks with a paper base. The paper base makes the entire stick compostable.

Reusable alternatives called ear picks are also available. There are several options like silicone, stainless steel, and bamboo. If you choose to purchase an ear pick, please be very careful, or you might damage your inner ear.

32. Toilet Paper

Americans flush 27,000 trees down the toilet every day. That is *a lot* of trees. Thankfully, you have a whole bunch of options to be less wasteful, but there's not a lot you can do when you're out of the house other than being conscious of how much TP you're using. Why people need a softball-sized amount of TP after a tinkle is really beyond me. One to two squares will do.

Bidet Attachment: My husband and I have managed to cut our toilet paper usage by 70 percent just by installing a bidet attachment to our toilet. Bidet attachments are relatively inexpensive costing $35–75.

A bidet attachment hooks up to the water supply near your toilet. There's a knob you turn to release fresh water to wash yourself after you go, and it's much more effective than just wiping.

Think about it . . . if a bird pooped on you, would you be OK with just wiping it off? If you went to pick up dog poop and got it on your hands would you just wipe it off? Of course not! You'd wash it off. Why not do the same for your butt?

We still use toilet paper to pat dry, but some bidet attachments come with really fancy fans to air dry your bum.

How to Buy Toilet Paper: When I buy toilet paper, I look for 100 percent recycled paper or tree-free paper made with bamboo or sugarcane pulp. I purchase my rolls individually wrapped in paper to avoid plastic.

The cardboard box the rolls come in, the paper wrapped around the rolls, and the TP core made from cardboard can all be composted in the backyard or recycled. I recycle the cardboard box and then compost the rest in my compost bin.

You can typically find plastic-free cases of toilet paper at an office supply store, or you can order them online. Several eco brands offer toilet paper in smaller cases like 12 and 24 rolls. It's a great option for those who don't have room to store a 48- or 96-roll case. Plus, you get to support an awesome company who's trying to make the world a better place.

A Note on Shipping: Shipping in itself isn't zero waste, but sometimes it's your only option. You have to remember that all of the products on store shelves were shipped in too. It's nice to buy in person simply because you can check the quality and make sure what you're buying is something you want, which prevents return shipments. When you're looking to make a purchase in-store or online, try to take note of where the product was made and try to support companies closer to home.

33. Tissues

I made the switch to handkerchiefs long before going zero waste. My dad always carried a handkerchief when I was growing up. Every year for Christmas, Santa would stuff a couple of new ones, typically embroidered with his initials, in his stocking.

When I first met my husband, one of the first things I noticed was that he always carried a handkerchief. I can honestly say, I haven't seen many guys in their twenties carry one around. On one of our dates, I asked him why he used a handkerchief. He said, "I have bad allergies, and handkerchiefs prevent my nose from chafing." "What magic is this!?" I thought and decided it was time to try out cloth handkerchiefs too.

Lo and behold, he was right. My nose hardly ever chafes anymore.

My beautiful collection of embroidered handkerchiefs were passed down from my great-grandmother, and I've picked up a few from estate sales around town. They're so intricate you almost feel guilty blowing your nose in them, but never fear, these hankies have withstood years of nose blowing. It's truly amazing how high-quality these pieces are—they're still around after 70 to 80 years. We just don't make things the way we used to.

The hardest part about switching to handkerchiefs is finding a good system. Handkerchiefs are small and can easily be misplaced. I use a porcelain tissue-box cover and stuff clean handkerchiefs inside.

Whenever my hankies are dirty, I toss them into the dirty

clothes hamper. I use handkerchiefs the most during allergy season. If I ever have the flu or a nasty cold, I'll place the hankies in a pot of water and bring them to a boil, hang them to dry, and then wash them with a regular load of clothes.

> **Estate sales are a fabulous place to find zero-waste items secondhand!**

34. Cotton Balls

If you use disposable cotton balls or cotton rounds to remove your makeup, use a washcloth or switch to reusable cotton rounds instead. If you've been using cotton balls or cotton pads to apply toner, put it into a spray bottle. Spritz the toner directly on your face, or spray it into your hands and apply it in a gentle upward motion. So much toner is absorbed by the cotton pads— by directly spraying it on, you can stretch the product and avoid wasting it.

35. Menstrual Products

There are several different options when it comes to having a zero-waste period. There are period panties, cloth pads, and menstrual cups—but first, let's talk about the problems with conventional products.

Conventional tampons and pads contain plastic (pads contain the equivalent of four plastic bags), and they're bleached to maintain their whiteness. Not only do you not want these things in such a sensitive area of the body, but they can also worsen cramps.

A tampon's job is to absorb blood, but unfortunately, it also absorbs all of your natural vaginal fluids, causing a pH imbalance which can lead to infections.

You're supposed to change your tampon every 4 to 8 hours and every time you go to the bathroom, which can add up to a lot of trash.

Menstrual Cups: Menstrual cups are a reusable alternative to tampons. They're made of medical grade silicone and catch your blood instead of absorbing it. Most cups catch two super tampons worth of blood, and they only have to be changed every 12 hours. When it's inserted correctly, you won't even know it's there. Plus, they can help relieve cramps. When the cup is unfurled, it rests against your vaginal wall, applying a slight amount of pressure that can reduce cramping.

When your menstrual cup is full, empty it while sitting on the toilet. If you have access to a private sink, you can rinse it out and reinsert. If you're in a public bathroom, you can wipe it with toilet paper, reinsert, and rinse it with water when you have the chance.

Boil your menstrual cup after your cycle to keep it clean.

> **A menstrual cup is one of my favorite zero-waste swaps I've made! My only regret is that I didn't start using one in college.**

Cloth Pads and Period Panties: If a menstrual cup isn't your style, check out cloth pads and period panties! I have a set of organic cloth pads and period panties that I enjoy using on medium and lighter days.

Cloth pads work infinitely better than their disposable counterparts. Cloth pads are softer and more comfortable, and you don't have to worry about rashes from synthetic materials. Cloth pads don't smell as bad either—just another example of inorganic and organic matter stinking when combined.

I have tried several period panties, and love them for lighter days. My go-to are Thinx. They're so comfy, as you don't have to deal with any bulk.

To clean both the cloth pads and the period panties after use, rinse them until the water turns clear. Hang them to dry, and once they're dry you can throw them in the hamper. Wash them in the washing machine, but do not tumble dry.

36. Razor

Instead of using a disposable plastic razor, switch to a stainless safety razor. At the end of the razor's life, you can recycle it fully, but beyond that, safety razors are meant to be repaired. They come apart completely for easy maintenance, and they all use the same type of blades whether it was a razor from the '50s or one made last week. (Yes, you can still buy functioning antique safety razors.)

Safety razors use a straight single blade. To shave, hold the razor at a 30-degree angle and use short strokes. There's no need to apply any pressure, simply let the razor glide across your skin.

I store my discarded blades in a blade bank. The blades are made from stainless steel, but you cannot put razor blades in your curbside bin. Recycling plants aren't completely automated, there are still people sorting the material by hand, and you don't want to endanger anyone working. To make a blade bank, you'll need a steel can. Opt for something like broth that contains no food particles. With an Exacto knife, you'll want to make an incision on the top of the can large enough for a blade to slide through. Drain all of the broth out of the can, and rinse with water. Leave upside down to dry for several days on a drying rack, and it's ready to use! Slip your discarded blades inside of the can. Once it's full, put a piece of tape over the opening and take it to your metal recycling facility. They'll be able to recycle it with machinery so no one will be hurt. Also, take a look at your waste management facility's website. Often they have special collection days for hazardous and dangerous and toxic items like razor blades, batteries, or e-waste.

On top of being better for the environment, switching to a safety razor has saved me a lot of money. I was buying a pack of razors two to three times a year for $20 each. My initial investment for my safety razor was $35. On average they run anywhere from $20–50, but you can also buy some very nice high-end ones. I also paid $10 for a pack of 100 blades. This $45 will last me for at least six years, resulting in a $255 savings.

Other zero-waste methods of hair removal include sugaring and laser hair removal. And, of course, you could always just not shave.

37. Skin-Care Routine

There is no one-size-fits-all skin-care routine. You will see this common theme throughout this section. Personal hygiene is just that—personal!

Skin care has been one the hardest things for me to master. I have spent a lot of money, a lot of time, and a lot of tears trying to find what works. I had perfectly clear skin until I turned 19. Once I hit 19, I got horrible cystic acne and skin congestion. It was full-blown all over my entire face, and nothing seemed to work. I tried everything, both store-bought and DIY. The only thing that cleared my cystic acne was focusing on healing my hormones after the breast cancer scare. I started paying really close attention to my cleaning products, beauty products, and diet. When I started changing my lifestyle, my cystic acne disappeared, but I still struggle with skin congestion, which is triggered by weather and water quality. After I moved to California four years ago, my skin's condition has been a mixed bag, thanks in part to low humidity and hard water.

I use a mix of DIY and store-bought products, but the most important thing for me has been looking at the ingredient list. Thankfully, most companies that are conscious of what's going in their products are also pretty conscious of how they're packaged.

Ingredients I'm Trying to Avoid

- **Parabens** are used as preservatives in products and are known endocrine disruptors that have been linked to breast cancer and reproductive issues.

- **Synthetic fragrances** are often in the ingredient list as "parfum" or "fragrance," which is code for an amalgam of different chemicals. Fragrances are considered trade secrets, so you really don't know what's in the mix you're spraying.
- **Artificial coloring** is made from coal tar and will be on the ingredient label as FD&C, D&C, or Red 6
- **Formaldehyde** is usually used in a water solution known as *formalin*. It's a preservative which keeps makeup and beauty products fresh over time. The downside is that it's known to cause cancer.
- **Toluene** is a petrochemical and used in paint thinner. It interferes with hormones and the immune system.

While any one of the ingredients might not cause harm in a very small amount, I wouldn't want to put any of them on my skin every day. Skin is our largest organ, and we should be careful what we put on it.

When you're researching skin-care products, the Environmental Working Group has a wonderful website where they rank products based on their ingredients to help you easily navigate the market.

To make my life easy, I buy from a beauty shop in San Francisco that does the homework for me. Everything on their shelves is vetted, and all of their products have to meet a long list of green beauty requirements. Several shops that have similar criteria are Credo Beauty, CAP Beauty, and the Detox Market; their products are available online.

When It Comes to Packaging

The first thing I look for is clear glass. Clear glass is more likely to be recycled than colored glass, but colored glass is still my close-second choice because glass can be recycled infinitely without any loss of quality.

I also look for pieces that can easily be taken apart for recycling. For example, if my skin-care bottle has a pump, can I remove all of the individual pieces and recycle them properly? Does the company offer a take-back program where they either sanitize and reuse or properly dispose of the bottles?

38. Lotion

Making lotion is a great DIY. Lotion tends to be a catch-all name for body moisturizers, but there are several different types, including lotion bars, liquid lotion, and body butter.

Body butter and lotion bars are both going to be shelf-stable because they don't have any water in them. What makes lotion is the addition of water. If you're buying lotion at the store, you know they had to use quite a few preservatives to keep it shelf-stable.

If you make lotion at home, you can keep it in the fridge for a month or two, but I try to opt for shelf-stable DIYs because it's not sustainable to make beauty products every couple of weeks unless it's something you really enjoy doing. I would much rather spend my time having fun not DIYing my skin care. Not to say DIYing isn't fun; it is! But, I don't want to be stuck doing it constantly. When I make products, I have a couple of ground rules:

1. I have to enjoy doing it
2. It has to be shelf-stable for at least six months
3. BONUS POINTS: If I can make a large batch and save it, or if the product has more than one purpose

If you feel the same way, you're going to love these recipes. You will also notice there isn't any coconut oil in my DIYs. Coconut oil takes a long time to absorb into the skin, it can leave you feeling greasy, and it can clog your pores. Having said that, fractionated coconut oil works well and absorbs into the skin more quickly, but it's difficult to find it without packaging.

LOTION BARS

Lotion bars are easy to carry with you on the go. The beeswax prevents the bar from becoming a melty mess. I buy my beeswax from a local beekeeper. I can buy a 1-pound block for $20 and 1 pound will last for years. You can substitute this with a vegan wax, but I haven't seen a place to buy any without packaging.

1 cup grated beeswax or beeswax pellets
2½ cups olive oil
Optional: Add a scent ingredient

1. Melt both ingredients over a double boiler. Once completely melted, add scent if using, pour the mixture into silicone molds, and let it rest at room temperature overnight.
2. In the morning you will have beautiful lotion bars ready to use. I store my lotion bars in a small tin.

> *Pro Tip:* Upcycled Altoids tins work great as lotion-bar holders! You can even pour the melted mixture straight into the Altoids tin. Once it's cooled, you'll just need to use the heat from your hands to really work the bar.

NON-GREASY BODY BUTTER

If you prefer slathering yourself in a cream rather than rubbing yourself with a bar, this is the DIY for you. Body butter is notoriously pretty greasy. This one is better, but it's still not going to be as smooth as a lotion.

The oils picked for this butter were specifically chosen for their absorbency rate. Every oil absorbs into the skin at a different rate, and I chose safflower oil because it's the fastest absorbing oil that's relatively inexpensive and can be commonly purchased in a glass bottle at most grocery stores.

¾ cup cocoa butter
¼ cup safflower oil

1. Melt both of the oils in a double boiler. Once they're melted, remove from the heat and place in the freezer. Once they're completely cooled, after about thirty minutes, whip the ingredients for several minutes with an electric mixer to incorporate air. It will become nice, fluffy, and double in size.

2. Cocoa butter is pretty stable in temperature, so it should maintain its fluffiness even in the summer months. If it starts to melt or collapse, you can always put it in the freezer and re-whip.

39. Deodorant

Deodorant is my original DIY, my cardinal sin that set me down the path of kitchen experiments and unlocked my inner mad scientist.

With my breast cancer scare came lots of pain. Depending on the day, it was difficult to manage, and a major factor in a lot of the lifestyle changes I was trying to make. As I was branching out into the world of DIY and natural living, I decided to start with deodorant.

If you're switching from conventional deodorant with an antiperspirant to a natural deodorant, you're going to want to do a detox (recipe below). After detoxing, you will find that you sweat less and that your sweat doesn't smell as bad. Sweat only stinks when it reacts with bacteria on the body. Sweating is good, and we shouldn't try to block our pores to prevent it.

After my initial detox and foray into DIY, the pain I had been struggling with vanished. I haven't had any pain in four years; my body was having an adverse reaction to the conventional antiperspirant deodorant.

Just because I accept sweating, doesn't mean I accept stinking. Here are a few of my favorite recipes.

PIT DETOX
The detox phase can take anywhere from three days to three weeks, but you can speed up the process by applying a detox mask to your armpits.

After doing this pit mask for three days, your detox process should be complete. Of course, everyone's body chemistry is different and it might take you a day or two longer. You might also want to repeat it occasionally. Around once a year, I'll still apply this detox mask to my armpits. This makes enough for one use.

1½ teaspoons activated charcoal
1½ teaspoons bentonite clay
1 tablespoon apple cider vinegar

Mix all of the ingredients together in a bowl. You might need to add a teaspoon of water to thin it out and make it more spreadable. Use your finger or a brush to apply the mask to your armpits. To avoid a giant mess, I would make this mask before jumping into the shower. Let the mask dry, hang out with your armpits up for 10 minutes, and then rinse off in the shower.

> **Don't forget: Don't use a metal spoon with bentonite clay! It will deactivate it.**

CHAMOMILE ACV ROLL-ON DEODORANT

Why it works: Apple cider vinegar prevents stinky sweat by killing any bacteria living on your armpits. ACV is acidic and discourages bacteria from setting up shop for the rest of the day. ACV can smell kind of like a salad, so I've found combining chamomile and ACV to be an effective and pleasant-smelling remedy.

You can double or triple this recipe, as you like.

½ cup raw apple cider vinegar

¼ cup chamomile flowers

1 cup water

1. Brew a strong cup of chamomile tea by steeping the flowers in one cup of boiling water for 5 minutes. Strain out the flowers and combine the chamomile tea and ACV.
2. I pour the mixture into a 1-ounce roll-on bottle, which I leave in my bathroom medicine cabinet for 2 to 3 weeks. I freeze the remaining liquid in an ice-cube tray and defrost when I need a new batch. A 1-ounce roll-on bottle is 2 tablespoons and most ice cubes are portioned at 2 tablespoons.

SEA SALT ROLL-ON DEODORANT

Salt is a powerful natural antibacterial. Using this roll-on deodorant makes your armpit an unhappy place for bacteria to live and makes you smell like the ocean.

1 teaspoon sea salt

2 tablespoons water

1. I like to run my salt through the blender so it becomes extra fine and powdery. This helps the salt dissipate and roll on evenly.
2. This DIY lasts 2 to 3 weeks in the fridge.

When using water in any DIY, it's always best to use filtered water and boil it for several minutes. Products made using water have a short shelf life because microbes and bacteria multiply in the water over time. We're not prolonging the shelf life of these products with a preservative, so we want to use filtered and boiled water to get the maximum shelf life, which is only a couple of weeks in the fridge.

NORMAL PERSON DEODORANT

I like this deodorant and call it "normal person" deo because you can add it to your old roll-up deodorant container. Of course, you could store this in a small jar, but I find it's much easier to apply when it's inside of a roll-up container. It glides on just like a store-bought deodorant and is super effective. It's what you might call "extra-strength."

3 tablespoons shea butter

2 tablespoons grated cocoa butter

3 tablespoons arrowroot powder

2 tablespoon baking soda

2–3 teaspoons vitamin E or safflower oil

1. Melt the grated cocoa butter using a double boiler. Once the cocoa butter has liquefied, add the shea butter. When the shea butter has liquefied, pull the mixture off the heat.

Add the baking soda and the arrowroot. Stir well to combine, making sure there are no lumps. Add in the vitamin E or safflower oil.

2. Pour into an old cleaned out deodorant container, and let it set at room temperature overnight. You can speed the process by placing it in the fridge for a couple of hours. Once it's set, it's ready to apply!

LEMON DEODORANT

This one is definitely out of the box, but it works! It's great if you have a lemon tree in your backyard or if you keep a lot of lemons in the house. You don't want the lemons to go bad while you're waiting to use them.

Take a slice of a lemon and rub it on your armpits! Like our first two DIYs, lemon juice is acidic and makes the armpits an unhappy place for bacteria. It's also high in citric acid, which helps to minimize pores and reduce sweating. Minimizing pores is fine; they're still open, and nothing is blocking them.

Note: Do not use lemons as a deodorant and then spend time in the sun or go sunbathing. When the sun interacts with the lemon juice, it can cause serious irritation.

40. Perfume

The number one ingredient in most perfumes is *parfum*. When I started looking at all of the endocrine disruptors in my life one of the first things to go was all of my perfume. I only kept the one bottle I had open. It's my absolute favorite, but I don't spray it on my skin. I only spray it on my clothes on special occasions. I don't want to spray it on my skin because I don't know what I'm spraying on my skin!

Don't get me wrong, I love to smell good, but I'm not going to compromise my health. All you have to do is a little research on your companies to make sure they're using organic ingredients and are free from synthetic fragrances, colors, phthalates, and parabens. You can always turn to a green beauty shop that does the homework for you, and thankfully most perfumes come packaged in glass—the bottles are beautiful and very easy to upcycle.

OR YOU CAN MAKE YOUR OWN PERFUME!

Most popular methods of making perfume use essential oil blends. You can find plenty of information for blending essential oils online, but I do things a little differently. I use rose petals, lavender petals, and chamomile flowers bought in bulk from my local tea shop. The blend is really mild and floral. You can infuse other types of herbs to get a different scent. You'll need a small 8-ounce swing-top jar to store the mixture in while it's being prepared, and a little roll-on bottle to strain it into once it's ready.

¼ cup dried rose petals

¼ cup dried lavender petals

¼ cup dried chamomile flowers

1 cup safflower oil

2 tablespoons vitamin E oil

1. Add the dried flowers to an 8-ounce swing-top jar. Pour the safflower oil over the flowers and close the jar. Place the jar on the windowsill and shake once a day for 2 to 3 weeks. The oil will be infused with a beautiful floral scent.

2. Strain the flowers out and pour the scented oil into a roll-on bottle.

3. Apply the scented oil to your hot spots. That's the wrist, behind the elbows, behind the knees, behind your ears, and where your collarbone meets in the middle.

41. Lip Balm

To make lip balm, I use a similar recipe to the lotion bars. I just pour this simple mixture into a small stainless tin with a screw-on cap. I also make a tinted version, which is nice for daily wear.

NON-TINTED LIP BALM
   1 tablespoon beeswax
   3 tablespoons olive oil

Melt the beeswax over the stove with a double boiler. Once it's completely melted, add the olive oil, and pour into a stainless tin with a screw-on lid. I like to use containers with a screw-on lid so you can throw the balm in your bag without worry.

TINTED LIP BALM
Alkanet is an herb that is found in the Mediterranean region and has been used for red dye since ancient times, and it's also used in Indian dishes like rogan josh.

   1 tablespoon beeswax
   3 tablespoons olive oil
   1 tablespoon alkanet root

Let the alkanet root and olive oil steep together for 7 to 10 days on the windowsill in a small glass jar. Strain the alkanet root out of the olive oil. It should be a bright pink color. Melt the beeswax over the stove with a double boiler. Once it's completely melted, add the tinted olive oil. Pour into a screw-top tin and let it cool.

42. Makeup

I have done my fair share of DIY makeup. As much as I love to DIY skincare, store-bought makeup lasts longer throughout the day. It's worth the splurge, and there are a lot of companies who are getting their ingredients and packaging right.

When it comes to packaging, I look for companies that package in glass, stainless steel, or bamboo. Several companies also offer refill programs, which are becoming popular: You purchase a really nice compact that has a small magnet in the back which holds a stainless steel refill tin. The small stainless tins have pressed eye shadow, blush, or foundation. Once you run out, you can order a new tin, which typically comes wrapped in a compostable paper pouch and place it in your old beautiful compact! The tins are made of very thin steel which you can recycle. It's a genius concept that saves a lot of packaging!

Mascara is by far the trickiest makeup item to find in sustainable packaging. Lush carries a mascara that comes in a glass jar with a plastic wand. The glass jar can be recycled, and you can clean the wand and send it to the Appalachian Wildlife Rescue— they use them to remove fly eggs and larvae from the fur of animals. Kjaer Weiss also has refillable mascara, packaged in stainless steel.

43. Hairspray

To give my hair a little bit of body, hold curl, or keep fly-aways in place, I spritz it with a little bit of DIY hairspray. Vodka helps the hairspray stay stable for a couple of months. Alcohol can dry out your hair, so if you are going to use this every day, I'd remove the vodka and store it in the fridge for a couple of weeks.

   1 orange, cut into wedges
   2 cups filtered water
   2 tablespoons sugar
   ¼ cup vodka

Boil the orange slices and press them down, allowing them to release their juices. Reduce the heat and simmer until the water has been reduced by half. Add the sugar and let it dissolve. Strain out the macerated oranges and pour the liquid into a spray bottle. Add the ¼ cup of vodka at the end.

44. Shampoo and Conditioner

Besides the plastic bottles they come in, many commercial shampoos contain endocrine disruptors like fragrance and parabens, and they strip away your natural oils. This causes your scalp to overproduce oils, requiring you to use more shampoo and buy more product.

Like with skin care, there is no one-size-fits-all solution for hair care so here are a couple of zero-waste options that are good for your hair and the planet. Some of the most popular options are no-poo, low-poo, shampoo bars, and buying shampoo in bulk.

The main point of going no-poo is that you stop using commercial shampoo products. Still, there are entire threads, chat rooms, and blogs solely dedicated to no-poo because there are so many different routines! If that's not your style, check with your closest health-food store or co-op—they probably have shampoo and conditioner available in bulk.

With no-poo and low-poo, your hair will go through a detoxing period as it experiences withdrawals from ingredients like silicone, which coats your hair for an artificial shine. For some people it's a couple of days, for others it can last a couple of months. As I started stretching time between washes, my detox period lasted for 2 to 3 weeks. After that, I could go a week without having to wash my hair, and in the middle of the week, I would use a homemade dry shampoo. Now my hair is softer, more manageable, and has fewer tangles. When using conventional shampoo my hair would become so knotted; I would spend 10 to 15 minutes just brushing every day! Thankfully,

I don't have to worry about that anymore. The detox period was worth the peace of mind I gained in knowing that I'm not interfering with my hormones, and I'm no longer hurting the environment.

A few tips when switching over:

1. Massage your scalp for a minute or two when your hair is dry before you go to bed. It's very relaxing, and it also helps to redistribute oil so you can go longer between washes.

2. Use a boar-bristle brush to help to redistribute the oils from root to tip. It will add natural shine.

> *Dry Shampoo Recipe:* **Use arrowroot powder if you have light-colored hair and arrowroot + cocoa powder if you have darker hair.**

NO-POO

There are a lot of different "no poo" solutions to hair care, but the most common is using a baking soda paste on the roots and then doing an acid rinse with a tablespoon of apple cider vinegar or white vinegar diluted in a cup of water.

LOW-POO

I participate in "Low Poo." Low Poo is washing your hair every couple of days with a shampoo that contains no sulfates and no silicones. I use Plaine Products which is sold in an aluminum bottle that can be sent back, sanitized, and refilled.

SHAMPOO BARS

Shampoo bars are another popular option. It's just shampoo concentrated in a bar form without water. They can be bought from local soap makers, you can DIY one, or you can even find them in some drugstores, grocery stores, and Lush. I've successfully used several shampoo bars, and there are a couple of tricks to using them.

1. Don't rub the bar on your head—especially not in your crown. Rub the bar together in your hands. Create a nice lather and then apply to your head.
2. Avoid concentrating the soap in your crown. In fact, I'd recommend shampooing the crown last. Since shampoo bars are so concentrated, they can leave behind soap build-up. They don't luxuriously rinse out of your hair like regular shampoo—you have to really scrub.
3. SCRUB! Give yourself a nice scalp massage—at least two minutes. Make sure you work all of the soap out of your hair.
4. Depending on the bar, your natural oil level, or whether you have soft or hard water, you might need to balance your pH with an acid rinse.

45. Exfoliation

Exfoliation is an important part of any skin-care routine. Dead skin can build up, clog your pores, and leave the skin looking dull.

Dry Brushing: Dry brushing helps to knock off dead skin cells and stimulate the lymphatic system. All you need is a brush with natural bristles. Start at the bottom of your feet with short strokes up your legs toward your heart. Then start with the bottom of your hands and brush toward your heart. Don't forget your back, chest, and tummy.

You don't need to press down super hard; a light brushing is fine. Brush in a counterclockwise motion, and the whole process should take 3-5 minutes. It's great to jump in the shower after you finish to wash away all of the skin cells you stirred up.

After you get out of the shower complete the ritual with a rub down of your homemade lotion bar.

Exfoliating Cleansers: When exfoliating your face you want to stay away from microbeads. Look for a cleanser that offers natural exfoliates like adzuki bean, cleansing grains, sugar, or salt.

If exfoliating every day is too harsh for your skin, you can whip up a few simple DIYs to use once or twice a week.

COFFEE SCRUB
The coffee grounds and brown sugar gently exfoliate. The caffeine from the coffee also brightens and tightens your skin. Safflower oil can unclog pores by combining with sebum, reduce rashes, and

reduce acne. It also promotes cell regeneration for younger look-ing skin. It's really the perfect oil to add to a DIY exfoliate. Plus, it's not too greasy, allowing you to wash free of it instead of lin-gering on your skin potentially clogging your pores or sink drain like coconut oil.

2 tablespoons coffee grounds
2 tablespoons brown sugar
1 tablespoon safflower oil
¼ teaspoon vanilla extract (completely optional!)

Mix together in a bowl. In the shower, turn off the water, and scrub all over your body. Makes enough for one use.

46. Body Wash

Instead of using body wash, swap to a good ol' bar of soap. You can typically find bars of soap with little to no packaging, even at the grocery store. If they do have packaging, they'll probably be wrapped in paper or a cardboard sleeve, both of which can be recycled or composted.

47. Shaving Cream

I am all about time-saving hacks, and I love it when my DIYs can pull double duty. It makes living zero waste more personally sustainable for me.

DIY SHAVING CREAM
   ¼ cup Non-Greasy Body Butter (page 85)
   2 tablespoons liquid castile soap

Whip the body butter and soap together. You'll get a creamy, foamy, luxurious, moisturizing, super-smooth shave!

If you prefer, you can avoid the DIY all together and opt for a nourishing bar of soap. You'll want to find a bar of soap with a lot of lather and look for nourishing oils that have a lower absorption rate, like shea butter and castor oil.

48. Face Masks

You're going to be ready for #selfcaresunday with these DIY face masks. There's something so relaxing and empowering about whipping together a face mask. It's like badass beauty meets mad scientist.

AVOCADO CUCUMBER MASK

Cucumbers and avocados are high in vitamin C, which help to brighten and smooth the skin. Avocados are also high in oleic acid which reduces redness and inflammation.

1 tablespoon avocado
1 tablespoon peeled cucumber

Mash the avocado and cucumber together with a mortar and pestle until a thick paste is formed. Evenly spread all over your clean, dry face. Let it sit for 10 minutes and then wash off with warm water.

SOOTHING AND MOISTURIZING

Matcha is full of antioxidants perfect for rejuvenation, tightening skin, and fighting free radicals. Raw honey is an antibacterial, which is great for acne prevention.

1 tablespoon matcha powder
1 teaspoon raw honey
2 teaspoons aloe vera gel

Stir all of the ingredients together and apply to a clean, dry face. Let it dry and leave it on 15 to 30 minutes. Rinse off with warm water and pat dry.

> **If you have dark or puffy under eye circles, apply a little bit of matcha mixed with water under your eyes while you're getting ready. Wash off after five minutes and say goodbye to puffiness!**

CHAPTER FOUR

CLEANING

Switching over to natural cleaning products is a breeze. All of these recipes contain ingredients you have lying around your kitchen. They're just as effective as the toxic cleaners from the store, and they're a fraction of the price. This is the zero-waste trifecta—good for your wallet, good for the planet, good for your health.

49. All-Purpose Cleaner

This is my favorite all-purpose cleaner. I use it on everything except granite and marble. I use it to wipe down wooden furniture, and it can also be used on floors, windows, the fridge, the toilet, the bathroom cabinets, and the list goes on. It really is an all-purpose cleaner.

DIY ALL-PURPOSE CLEANER

- 1 part warm water
- 1 part white vinegar (bought in a glass bottle at the grocery store)

Mix together in a spray bottle.

> Many glass bottles like soy sauce, vinegar, and hot sauce that have small openings can be turned into cleaning bottles. You can buy spray nozzles from your local home improvement store to upcycle your leftover bottles into green cleaning machines.

50. Granite and Marble Countertop Cleaner

If you have a granite or marble, you'll want to avoid using vinegar or alcohol because it can scuff or etch the countertop. Instead, opt for a gentle cleaner like the one below.

EASY CLEANER FOR GRANITE AND MARBLE
   1 tablespoon liquid soap, like Dr. Bronner's Pure
      Castile Soap
   1 cup water

Mix together in a spray bottle.

51. Deodorizing Spray

Vodka is a disinfectant and will kill bacteria-causing odors. You can spray this mixture on your carpets, bedding, curtains, or clothing! I spray clothes after I've worn them and let them air out to extend the time between washes.

DIY HOME DEODORIZER
  1 part vodka
  1 part filtered water

Pour both ingredients into a spray bottle and shake well. You don't need full-strength vodka to get the job done, and you also don't need nice vodka. Go for the cheapest one that comes in a glass bottle.

52. Carpet Deodorizer

If you need something a little heavier for stinky shoes or a musty carpet, try this method. Baking soda and cinnamon are odor-absorbing powerhouses!

EASY CARPET DEODORIZER
    1 part cinnamon powder
    2 parts baking soda

1. Fill up an old spice jar a third of the way with cinnamon, and fill the other two-thirds with baking soda.
2. Sprinkle this mixture on the carpet or in your shoes and let it sit for at least four hours. Vacuum it up and repeat as many times as needed.

53. Room Deodorizer

If you have people coming over and want your house to smell amazing, try this method.

QUICK ROOM DEODORIZER
- ½ cup white vinegar
- 1½ cups water
- 3 cinnamon sticks

In a pot, bring all of this to a rolling boil. Turn down the heat and let it simmer for five minutes. Move the pot to any room in the house that needs a little bit of a boost.

> To keep the air in your home purified, purchase houseplants from a local nursery, or check for them on Craigslist or a local Freecycle group. Lots of people sell or give away houseplants when they move. Common houseplants that specialize in air purification are aloe vera, peace lily, spider plant, devil's ivy, philodendron, and areca palm.

54. Tub and Toilet Cleaner

This is my favorite cleaning recipe! It is seriously MAGIC!!

DIY TUB AND TOILET CLEANER
- ¾ cup baking soda (bought in bulk)
- 2–3 tablespoons hydrogen peroxide
- 2–3 tablespoons liquid castile soap

Mix all of these ingredients in a small bowl. The mixture should become a thick paste. With a bamboo scrub brush, rub the paste onto the area. Let it sit for 10 minutes and then easily wipe the grime away.

> **This makes a great oven cleaner too! Apply, and let it sit for 1 to 2 hours, then spray with straight vinegar to activate the baking soda. Let it fizzle out and then get your scrub on.**

55. Glass Cleaner

Cleaning your windows and mirrors with a natural cleaner requires a different process than when you use a commercial cleaner.

I use the all-purpose vinegar cleaner from page 108. Spray the cleaner onto a 100 percent cotton rag with a wide weave. Use the dampened rag to wipe down the glass. Then follow with a completely dry cotton rag. This will leave your windows and mirrors with a streak-free shine.

If you're still experiencing streaks, make sure your cotton rags are lint-free and fully absorbent. Run them through a rinse cycle in the washing machine with vinegar to release any soap that might be built up inside of the fibers, keeping them closed and unable to absorb more cleaner.

56. Floor Cleaners

SIMPLE HARDWOOD AND LAMINATE FLOOR CLEANER

When mopping your hardwood floors, you do not want to soak the floor with this solution. Soaking the floors can cause water to seep between the boards, which can lead to warping.

Just a light sprinkling will do. This is more about elbow grease.

½ cup white vinegar
1½ cup water

Add both ingredients to a spray bottle. You can lightly spray the floors or spray this directly onto your cotton mop pad.

> *Pro Tip:* Use an old lonely sock as a cotton cover for your Swiffer!

DIY SLATE AND TILE FLOOR CLEANER

Unlike hardwood floors, tile floors don't mind a little water.

2 gallons very hot water
¼ cup liquid soap, like Dr. Bronner's

Combine both ingredients into a large bucket and use a cotton janitor-style mop. Use an old toothbrush to work on the grout.

57. Hand-Washing Dish Soap

You can use just liquid castile soap to hand wash your dishes, but the washing soda offers a little bit of scouring power and helps soften the water so you're left with streak-free glasses.

DISH SOAP

   1 cup of boiling water
   ½ cup of Dr. Bronner's liquid castile soap
   1 tablespoon of washing soda

Fill a kettle, place it on the stove, and bring it to a boil. Pour a cup of boiling water into a large glass measuring cup and dissolve a tablespoon of washing soda in it. Once it's dissolved, add the liquid soap, and pour the mixture into a soap dispenser. Give it a really good shake before using. If the soap becomes too thick, add a little bit more water.

Did you know you can easily make washing soda? All you need to do is place baking soda on a shallow baking sheet and heat it to 400 degrees. I leave mine in the oven for an hour and stir once halfway through.

Baking soda is sodium bicarbonate and washing soda is sodium carbonate. When you heat the baking soda you change the chemical structure by releasing excess carbon dioxide.

58. Dishwasher Detergent

Using a dishwasher actually saves more water than hand washing. The average Energy Star dishwashing machine only uses 4 gallons of water, and the average flow rate of a kitchen sink is 2.2 gallons per minute. Yikes! So save water and run the washing machine. To make it even more eco-friendly, make sure the dishwasher is completely full.

2 teaspoons coarse sea salt
2 teaspoons baking soda
½ teaspoon of Hand-Washing Dish Soap (page 116)

This only makes enough for one load. You can premix your baking soda and sea salt to streamline things and then just add a pump of the Hand-Washing Dish Soap before you press the start button.

> If you have hard water, you might still have water spots. I keep my glasses streak free and clean them the same way I clean windows, using the technique on page 114.

59. Laundry Detergent

I don't recommend replacing laundry detergent with a DIY option. Most homemade laundry detergent is really laundry soap, which can clog your washing machine, void the warranty, and ruin your clothes. I used homemade laundry soap before I went zero waste and ruined a set of sheets and several items of clothing with built-up soap residue. (This might also be the culprit for why your cotton towels aren't absorbing water! The oils in the soap build up on fabric over time, making it water resistant.) Thankfully, I didn't ruin the washing machine.

I don't recommend soap nuts or chestnuts for the same reason. Both of these items contain saponin or soap. This will cause soap buildup on fabric, preventing it from being absorbent, and the residue can cause skin irritation. Historically, people used soap to clean their clothes, but they washed their clothes by hand. The agitation process was harsh enough for the soap to wash clean. Our modern washing machines aren't as rigorous so the soap clings to the fabric.

If you can't buy laundry detergent in bulk, opt for a powder in a cardboard box and make sure the detergent you're buying is biodegradable! I prefer Seventh Generation. When going to recycle the box, open it all the way up so it's flat, and shake out all of the remaining powder.

60. Dryer Balls

To make clothes nice and fluffy, you can use dryer balls. Dryer balls separate clothing, allowing more air to circulate, which results in a faster drying time. You can buy wool dryer balls or you can easily make your own.

My method is a little unconventional, as it starts with a 100 percent wool sweater from the thrift store. The goal is to cut the sweater into pieces and form them into softball-size spheres.

First, cut several large circular shapes around 8" in diameter. You'll want to fill each circle with wool scraps. Wrap the scrap pieces inside of the circle and stitch the circle shut at the top with a needle and thread, creating a sphere.

Throw the wool spheres in with your next load of laundry. Wash and dry them two to three times until the wool has completely felted.

If you really want your spheres to be perfectly round, you can unravel the sweater and start from yarn, and ball it until it's roughly the size of a softball.

61. Air Drying

Putting your clothes in the dryer can wear them out quickly. Each time you dry, micro tears are created in the fibers. This shortens the life span of the clothing and can distress the garment's shape. Instead, opt for a super–environmentally friendly way of drying your clothes: hang them to dry with wind and sun power! On a warm sunny day, sheets can be dry in an hour or two.

You don't have to have anything fancy to dry your clothes outside. In the backyard, I tied a rope between a tree and a fence post. I also have a bamboo drying rack, which I can use to dry inside, and when the weather's nice, I put the rack out in the sun. It worked great when I was living in an apartment with a small balcony.

62. Natural Bleach Alternative DIY

This homemade substitute for bleach is safe for all colors. I've even used this method on white silk. Don't wring the silk after applying the bleach to it or rinsing it—just gently press the water out. The lemon juice, the peroxide, and the sun pack a three, two, one punch of whitening power.

NATURAL BLEACH

Juice of 1 lemon

1 cup 3 percent hydrogen peroxide

1 tablespoon liquid soap, like Dr. Bronner's Pure Castile Soap

1 gallon very hot water

In a two-gallon bucket, mix all of the ingredients and submerge your stained items. Let them soak for 15 minutes. After 15 minutes the water should be cool enough to agitate the clothes. Agitate them and let them sit for a couple of hours. Ring them out under cool running water and hang to dry in the sun.

63. Stain Removal Guide

The trick to stains is catching them fast.

- Ink stains: Apply rubbing alcohol to the stain and blot.
- Chocolate and blood stains: Soak the stain in a bowl containing 1 part 3-percent hydrogen peroxide and 1 part water for 5 minutes, and then rinse.
- Lipstick and oil stains: Apply dish soap to the stain; agitate and rinse with water. Follow with a vinegar and water rinse.
- Wine: Put a little 3-percent hydrogen peroxide on a white rag and blot the stain. Wait 5 minutes and rinse with cool water. Repeat as needed.

CHAPTER FIVE

BECOMING A CONSCIOUS CONSUMER

The best way to prevent waste from leaving your home is to prevent it from entering your home. It all starts with shopping. First, we'll evaluate our resources and redistribute them in more useful ways, and then we'll rebuild our shopping habits to prevent major cleanouts in the future.

64. Make Room for the Things You Care About

I'm going to guess that you probably have a little too much stuff. Maybe it's a closet stuffed with a few too many clothes. Maybe a drawer full of linens that's a little too difficult to close. Maybe it's a basement or garage you've dreaded cleaning out.

Americans tend to overconsume. We buy a lot of stuff that we never use or use only a few times and shove in an organizing bin to be forgotten. We buy this stuff because we make rash purchasing decisions. Maybe the decision was fueled by a sale, or the item was cute, or it was adequate for the moment. We have a problem with buying things we don't really love and things we don't really need. This stuff sits untouched until the next clean-out. It doesn't bring us happiness; no emotions are evoked when we look at it. It's just filling space.

Living a zero-waste lifestyle is about living with what you need—living with things that add value to your life. It's about truly *enjoying* the things you have. It's not about living without stuff. It's about carefully choosing the stuff that surrounds you.

I want to encourage you to go through your belongings and do a massive clean-out. Living a zero-waste lifestyle isn't about hoarding and holding onto everything you own. It's about living a simpler life and having the time to focus on the things that you truly care about. You are much more likely to take care of the belongings you own if you truly love them. Caring and maintaining our belongings is a very important part of reducing waste.

Now, when I recommend that you clean out your belongings, I'm not advocating that you take them to the landfill. No, this is about taking the resources you currently own and redistributing them. It's about putting items that are unused back into the world so they can be used, loved, and cherished by someone else. When you redistribute your resources, you're preventing new resources from being extracted. You're helping to fuel the secondhand market, which keeps current resources in play longer and prevents new resource production.

As you go through all of your belongings, separate them into four main piles: Keep, Use-Up, Donate, and Trash.

I want you to go through every cupboard, drawer, dresser, attic, and basement area that you have. You will come up with a mountain of stuff. In fact, you'll probably find a lot of stuff you didn't even know you had. It's crazy to really look at all of the things you own. If pulling out all of your stuff feels overwhelming, go a little slower. Go cabinet by cabinet or drawer by drawer. Really spend time with your belongings. Maybe even journal about it. Try to pay attention to your feelings, and most importantly, learn to separate your feelings from your belongings.

Some questions to consider:

- Is it necessary?
- Where/who did it come from?
- How much did you spend on it?
- How often do you use it?
- Does it add value to your life?
- Do you use it on a weekly basis?
- Do you love it?
- Could someone else use it more than you?
- If you were shopping today, would you buy it again?

Some items will clearly fall into one category or another. Some will fall into a Maybe zone. Try to have as few Maybes as possible. My recommendation for the Maybe pile is to box it up and put it away for thirty days. If you don't think about anything in that box for thirty days, don't open it! Just donate it.

What to Keep

Most organizational books will tell you to find what you don't like and get rid of it, but I personally find that it's better to start with what you love. We feel pretty ambivalent about most of our things. But, there are a few items that stick out that we absolutely LOVE. Start with what you love—not like, LOVE. Like all-caps LOVE. These are the things you keep. Everything else should be on the chopping block.

Of course, we also have to keep the things that we need. The washing machine certainly does not excite me and doesn't inspire any amount of all-caps LOVE or lowercase love, but I do like clean clothes . . . and not smelling bad. Make sure that you're taking the necessities into account as well.

What to Use Up

Don't go crazy and start throwing away every half-used box of aluminum foil or half-empty bottle of shampoo. Like we talked about in Tip 24, throwing out items is in contradiction to a zero-waste lifestyle. But I completely understand if you don't feel comfortable using your current products on your skin, home, or around your food. Maybe they're full of toxins you don't feel safe interacting with anymore. In this case, I would see if a friend or family member who buys those products would use them. There's nothing wrong with passing them along, especially since they were going to buy these items anyway. Gifting them is better than landfilling them. This reduces the amount of new resources we use, even if by a tiny amount.

What to Donate

Everything in this pile should be of high quality. But I don't recommend dropping everything off at your local thrift store. Most of the items we bag up and drop off at our local donation centers will never see store shelves. There's just too much stuff. There's not enough manpower to sort everything, and most items aren't in good enough condition to sell. A lot of our donations are shipped off to developing countries or landfilled. Unwanted clothing is sent in bulk to countries that don't have the proper waste management facilities to deal with the excess. Not only is this dangerous from an environmental standpoint, but it also depresses the value of local goods.

Instead, follow the hierarchy of donations below.

The Hierarchy of Donations

FRIENDS

Friends are always my first stop, but you have to make sure they want it and will use it. Never force an item onto a friend. When I was downsizing, I had to donate a lot of items. I had a Margaritaville machine that I loved . . . and I mean LOVED, but it was rarely used. It was a huge kitchen appliance that was relegated to the back of the cabinet. It took forever to get out and set up. I didn't have the space for it so I rarely used it. In fact, whenever I was making margaritas, I made them on the rocks because the Margaritaville was just too painful to set up. It was a waste of resources in my possession. It was a brand-new, good-quality, expensive piece of machinery collecting dust in the cabinet. I knew it could be better served elsewhere.

One of my good friends had just bought a gorgeous bar for their house. I knew exactly what that bar was missing . . . a Margaritaville. I called them up to see if they'd be interested in taking the machine off my hands. They were thrilled! As a bonus, I can head over to their house for a margarita any time.

Giving items to friends is at the top of the list because if you need them for some reason, you can typically borrow them. It's like still having access to the items without having to store them. It's the best of both worlds.

SELL

It's always much easier for me to part with an item if I know I can make a little bit of money off of it. You have a couple options: you can go the traditional garage sale/yard sale route or hone in on specific items.

When I downsized, I didn't have enough stuff to justify a yard sale. Most of my high-end, expensive items were designer clothes, and clothes don't typically do well at yard sales. Instead, I took my designer duds to a local consignment shop, and they took care of everything for me. I didn't have to worry about listing items or taking photos. It was a hands-off process. They made everything so simple, and I was cut a check when my items sold.

If you have the patience and time, you can always sell individual items yourself. Collector items can be listed on eBay. You can also list larger, more specific items like furniture or appliances on Craigslist.

SPECIFIC CHARITIES

Instead of boxing up all your stuff and dumping it at your local thrift store, look for charities or nonprofits that take specific items. It's a great feeling to redistribute your resources and play an active part in supporting your local community!

- Leftover building materials or furniture? Contact your local Habitat for Humanity. They can use these materials for their projects or sell them in their resale store to raise money for their projects.
- Bedding, towels, newspapers, or a lot of shredded paper? Call your local animal shelter; they're always in need of these items.
- Extra feminine hygiene products? Check with your local homeless or women's shelter. They are often in desperate need of these items.
- Nice work wear or suits? Stores like Men's Warehouse run yearly suit drives to collect suits for men and women who are looking to enter into the workforce. Also, check with homeless shelters as they often have programs to prepare and provide attire for job interviews.
- Gently used makeup? Check with your local women's shelter. They often supply makeup to the women going on job interviews, or you can send to Project Beauty Share.
- Too many arts and crafts supplies? A musical instru-

ment you haven't played in a while? Donate these items to your local school's art departments.

- One too many old prom dresses? Wouldn't it be awesome to give that dress to a girl whose family might not be able to afford a prom dress? There are often charitable organizations or schools running these programs every spring.
- Too many books weighing you down? Donate them to your school library, public library, or local prison (paperbacks only!).

I guarantee, any item you have, there is someone out there who wants it. It's just a quick Internet search or phone call away.

THRIFT STORE

Any items you still have left over can be taken to your local thrift store drop off location. Use this as a last resort.

Trying to find specific charities to donate to will be a little more time-consuming. It's certainly not as easy as just dropping all of the stuff off at Goodwill, but your stuff is actually going to be used! And, honestly, a little bit of pain is a good thing. We live in a society full of convenience. Everything is one click away, and it's on our doorstep tomorrow. We live in an instant society where over-consumption is not only encouraged, it's expected.

When you feel the pain of redistributing all of your stuff, you'll seriously analyze every purchase you make from here on out. You'll think long and hard before you go through this process again.

Letting Go When It's Hard

Sometimes, you have items you know you don't need. These items aren't useful. They don't enrich your life, but something inside just won't let you let go. This can be for numerous reasons. Maybe they were a gift. Maybe they belonged to a relative who passed. Maybe the items make you feel connected to a memory, a person, or a moment in time. How do you let go when these things keep you connected?

Growing up, I used to hoard paper and gifts. Even if the gift was something I hated, I couldn't bear to get rid of it. This gift was a physical representation of love. It bound me to the other person for all of eternity, so I must store it somewhere special . . . where it will never be looked upon or used . . . but it will be there just in case I need a reminder of their love.

Do those feelings sound familiar?

I had an entire closet filled with this stuff that I didn't use or like! Then one day, I had this wonderful realization. I was 21 and living in Austria. I was hanging out with one of my friends and we stumbled into a shop where I found a scarf that I loved. I decided not to buy it because I didn't need it. We kept walking, poking our head into shops while making our way to the Salzach River with two beers and a pretzel to split. While we were sitting on the bank of the river, I lamented about not buying the scarf, and she said something that has stuck with me to this day: "It's just stuff. It's just things."

My mind was blown. How had I not connected this simple principle to all of my stuff and all of my things?

Your memories do not live in your stuff.

Your relationships do not live in your stuff.

Your love is not represented by stuff.

You are not your stuff.

When I got home, I was able to finally clean out that closet. It was all just stuff. It was all just things. You have to separate the emotion from stuff. Stuff is not emotional. These emotions live inside of you.

Help! I'm Still Overwhelmed

This item was a gift. The job of a gift is to be received. Did you receive it? If so, your work is done. You own that gift, and as its rightful owner, you decide what happens to it next. Relinquish yourself from all guilt. You already accomplished the goal.

This item is a family heirloom. Is there another family member who wants? If it's just collecting dust in an attic, what good is it? Could it bring joy to someone else? If so, maybe it's time to pass it on to someone else's family.

This item connects me to someone who's passed. If you're not using it, I'm not sure what good it's doing. Your relationship goes so much deeper than just an item. An item won't bring them back.

Tips and Tricks

I'm not against holding onto things that are special to you and invoke memories. I myself have a shoebox full of playbills from shows I've been in and seen. Just make sure not to go overboard. Limit yourself to one or two boxes so you don't wind up with an attic full of "memories."

When you're letting go of something, you can journal about it. If you have a strong connection to an item, sometimes it's nice to get it all out on paper. Write about the item. Write about the memories it invokes. Whenever you're feeling nostalgic, flip through the pages of your journal. You can keep all of the thoughts without a physical item taking up space.

You can also take photos of the items. Take pictures of everything you love and store it in a book, picture box, or external hard drive. Whenever you're feeling sentimental, you can flip through all of the photos, and experience all of the emotions without holding onto extra stuff.

65. How to Purchase

Now that you've gone through all of your possessions, it's important to reframe your thinking for the future. Going through all of your items is not an excuse to run out and fill every empty drawer with new items. Every new thing that crosses the threshold of your doors should hold significance and weight.

Enjoy the breathing room. Learn to love the space. Learn to love the freedom. The more stuff we have, the more it owns us— the more it weighs us down. After letting go of all the excess, you should feel lighter. You should feel happier. Instead of having hundreds of items grabbing for your attention, you have the freedom to focus on the things you truly care about.

When we truly love things, we are so much more likely to take care of them. Zero waste is not about deprivation. I repeat: It is NOT about deprivation. Zero waste is a tool to you can use to frame your purchasing decisions.

Buying stuff is not evil. There's nothing wrong with buying stuff. The problem is in the way we consume. First of all, we overconsume. Secondly, we're overconsuming the wrong stuff. The stuff we're buying isn't well-made and is manufactured with the landfill in mind.

A lot of our everyday products are made in areas with little regulation. The workers are underpaid, safety is not a priority, and waste management infrastructure doesn't exist, creating toxic working and living environments for the surrounding communities.

These items are then shipped halfway around the world to the US in an ocean freightliner. Once they dock at the port, the goods are trucked across the country to your local store where you pick them up, bring them home, and then toss them into your 64-gallon trash can after only a short while. We have become very detached from our supply chain, and that has to change.

> **When making a purchase, ask yourself: Who made this? Do I support that? Where did this come from? Can I repair this? What's going to happen to this after I'm through with it?**

It can be really overwhelming when you start digging into the supply chain and learn the story behind your stuff. But you have to remember—when it comes to making purchases in this linear economy; there is no such thing as a perfect decision. At this moment in time, it doesn't exist. All you can do is make the best decision about what to buy in your particular situation, in whatever moment you're in.

Buy Nothing

Do you really need the item you're about to buy? Think long and hard before making any purchase. I like to reference the flowchart on page 3.

The flowchart is designed to prevent unnecessary purchases, but occasionally one or two will make their way to the end. I remember preparing for Thanksgiving 2015—my second time hosting everyone. At the time, I didn't have a potato masher. I remembered how much I wanted a potato masher in 2014. Mashing all those potatoes with a fork was unpleasant.

So, I followed the flowchart.

Do I need it? Yes.

Will I use it more than once a week? I love mashed potatoes. I make them at least once a week.

Can it serve more than one purpose? Yes, I can mash potatoes, avocados, chickpeas, egg salad, cauliflower, stewed tomatoes, the list goes on.

Is it unique? A fork just cannot do the job as efficiently.

Will it enrich your life? Yes!

I received the flowchart's stamp of approval, and I bought a potato masher. Not just ANY potato masher, though: it was sturdy and well-made, and every time I look at that potato masher, I feel happy.

Yes, I'm giddy at the sight of a potato masher. You know why? Because I waited. I thought about it. It was something I needed. I was so involved in this purchase that now I'm happy every time I see my potato masher. Every purchase you make should make you giddy. Even something as simple as a potato masher.

When you're invested in the supply chain, and you're truly thinking about your belongings, the small stuff brings you joy. Imagine what it would be like if every item in your space surrounded you with this much happiness. I can tell you from personal experience that it's life-changing.

66. Where to Purchase

Secondhand

The only thing better than not buying anything at all is to buy something that's already been bought. When you're shopping the secondhand market, you aren't sucking up any new resources to meet your needs.

The secondhand market is full of useful items. Almost every piece of furniture, clothing, kitchen gadget, and electronic I own is secondhand. Not only is it cheaper, but you can't tell the difference between these items and brand-new ones. Most of the items I've found secondhand still have the tags on them or are unopened in their original boxes. Most people have too much stuff, and they're looking to off-load it just like you were when you started cleaning out. These items are in great condition, but the owners no longer have a need for them.

I would always encourage you to look at the secondhand markets first for items you need. You'll be surprised by what you can find. Check out local thrift stores for hidden treasures, or look online for very specific purchases. Craigslist has a number of local secondhand treasures as well as lists of weekly garage and estate sales. And you can check out eBay for homewares, clothes, and electronics. I also like thredUP for clothing since you can search for specific clothing items.

Don't forget to ask friends and family members too! Whenever I'm looking for something specific, I'll call up friends and family to see if they have an extra one lying around. I always offer to buy it, but most of the time, if they have it, they just give it to me for free.

Shop Local

If you can't find what you're looking for on the secondhand market, look for something locally made. When you're looking in your area, you're supporting your local economy, and you can ensure the quality. It's so much easier to check out something when you can see and feel it rather than judging from a picture online.

It also saves on carbon miles. Think of all the resources used to transport our goods halfway around the world. I especially apply this principle to consumable goods. You shop for consumables more than anything else—things like food, beverages, soap, etc. But, my principle also includes specialty shops run by local artisans and craftspeople like cobblers and tailors.

Most of these shops aren't going to have a large online presence. At least, they don't in my town. I discovered most of these shops while on foot or asking someone who seems to know everything about the city. Do you have a friend that knows the ins and outs of your town? Ask them if they know someone with chickens for eggs or goats for milk. Ask if they know someone who makes soap, or where to get your dress hemmed, or your shoes resoled.

Always check locally. I bet someone in your town can help you out with what you're looking for.

Ethical and Sustainable

If no one in your town is able to help you, it's time to look elsewhere. The Internet brings so many people together with common goals. There are tons of zero-waste business popping up each and every day. There are also awesome shops on Etsy where you can customize almost anything to your liking.

This does involve shipping. Shipping in itself isn't zero waste, but sometimes it's your only option. We don't live in that perfect circular economy. We can only do the best we can where we are.

When you're looking for products, make sure these products align with your values. Ask yourself: How are these products made? Are they made in an ethical way? Are these products made with the environment in mind? Is this business supporting a closed-loop process? Will this product help me lead a more sustainable life? Is this object meant to be repaired? Where is this product going after I'm through with it?

Unsustainable, but Made to Last

This is the least desirable option on the list, but sometimes it's the only way. If you have to buy something that doesn't align with your values, make sure it's going to last a long, long time. Reducing your frequency of purchases is one of the best things you can do for the planet. If you have to buy something unsustainable, make sure you never have to purchase that item ever again.

Of course, it's easy to talk in such black-and-white terms, but it's more difficult when you actually have to live it day-to-day. Really, the best thing I can ask of you is to make the best decision you can in whatever situation you're in. Living zero waste is not about perfection; it's about making better choices. Being an informed consumer is 95 percent of the battle. As long as you're making informed decisions and you're aware of what you're purchasing and where it comes from, you're doing great!

67. A Note on Shipping

Shipping can have a lot of waste associated with it from the carbon miles to the polystyrene packing peanuts.

The best thing you can do is speak up. Make your packaging requests known. During an online transaction, there's typically a place for notes to the seller. You can request plastic-free shipping. Ask for paper tape and brown paper. Make sure to emphasize no plastic. Most of the time they'll honor your request.

I'm going to hope they honored your request. Now you have brown paper, which is recyclable, and a box, which is also recyclable. But, here are some more ideas. Recycling is energy intensive and not a perfect solution. We should look to reuse our items before recycling them.

Brown Paper
- Wrap presents with it
- Cut it up for grocery lists
- Use it for scratch paper or drawings
- Use it to ship another package
- Bring it to work if they have a shipping department
- Bring it to a UPS Store or other shipping store which will reuse packing materials
- Compost it
- Recycle it

Box
- Ship something else in it or package up a gift
- Use it as a storage container

- Offer it to someone who is moving
- Find a local business that needs boxes for shipping
- Use it for a school project or arts and crafts
- Recycle it

If your item came wrapped in a plastic bag or film, go to plasticfilmrecycling.org and find your nearest location to recycle film. You can't usually recycle this stuff curbside, but most grocery stores have a location at the front where you can recycle your old plastic bags and plastic films.

If you wind up with loads of Styrofoam peanuts, bubble wrap, or other undesirable packing materials, salvage what you can and take them to a UPS Store or other shipping location and they will re-use them. While this isn't a perfect option, at least you're reusing something. If everyone kept reusing packing peanuts, it would lessen the demand for new peanuts to be manufactured.

CHAPTER SIX

WORK, SCHOOL, AND OUT TO EAT

Many of our workplaces create waste entirely out of our control. That doesn't mean we still can't look for ways to combat waste in small daily actions.

68. The Fountain Pen

Switching to a fountain pen has been one of my favorite swaps. I always keep two fountain pens and a bottle of ink on my desk at work. Writing with a fountain pen is so smooth. I always thought a fountain pen wasn't for me because I'm left handed, but I was so wrong. It's the best writing utensil I've ever had. Writing with a fountain pen changes the grip where your hand is below the pen instead of beside/on top of it. No more ink all over my pinky! (Left-handed readers, you understand the ink-on-pinky plight.)

Fountain pens come with cartridges or converters. Cartridges have ink already in them. You have to keep buying them for your pen, and it creates quite a bit of unnecessary waste. Instead, look for pens with converters. Whenever you're running low on ink, you can easily refill the pen yourself from a bottle of ink. This is much cheaper than buying cartridges, and it creates less waste. Ink comes in a glass bottle, so once it's empty, you can recycle it.

69. Recycled and Double-Sided Paper

You might not be able to control what type of paper your office buys, but for your home office, buy paper made from 100 percent recycled content.

Find the settings on your computer to make sure you're printing double-sided. You can also change your font to conserve ink. Garamond, Times New Roman, and Helvetica are good choices.

70. The Trash Can

If you have a trash can at your desk and someone other than yourself empties it, I can almost guarantee that it's not being sorted. Whenever you have recycling, don't throw it in your desk trash can, walk it to the recycling bin. As a bonus, this encourages you to get up and get some exercise!

I always have a lot of paperwork on my desk, so I've been able to switch my under-the-desk trash can for a recycling bin. If you're in a similar situation, chat with the janitorial staff; they might have designated blue bins for recycling and be able to make the swap.

71. Being Prepared with Reusables

I'm very fortunate that my office has a small kitchen with a microwave, toaster oven, real plates, real mugs, and real flatware.

My office is very supportive of green initiatives. The recycle bins at work say, "Recycle or die." I'm always amazed how being your authentic self influences others around you. I watched so many people opt for real plates and real flatware in lieu of paper plates and plastic flatware simply because they saw from my zero-waste practice how easy it was.

Sometimes, you have to be the example.

In the office kitchen, we have room to store other items, like tiffins, tea strainers, reusable straws, olive oil, etc. If you don't have this space, you might think of storing some items at your desk to have on hand.

72. Office-wide Initiatives

Depending on how large your office is, think of all the amazing changes you could make. Does your office have a sustainability team that works on special projects? The company I work at isn't big enough to have one, but several of my friends serve on their company's sustainability team. Their job is to introduce eco initiatives and help publicize them throughout the company. They're tasked to come up with simple changes and break it down into super simple steps for everyone to join. Along the way they might even save the company some money; saving resources tends to save money too.

My friend got a sign placed in the cafeteria asking people to think twice about using a straw, and they saw a massive reduction in straw usage. One of my friends got a compost bin installed at work so all of their food scraps could be diverted from the landfill. Even small things like this add up to a huge impact! See if there are any office-wide initiatives you could come up with at your company.

I recommend that people start with a simple sorting presentation. Show the other employees what is and isn't recyclable in your city. Then place signs above the recycle bin with pictures of what is recyclable! This will help people easily identify what to put in each bin.

73. Pack Your Lunch

Lunchtime can be super wasteful if you're used to grabbing take out or prepackaged snacks. The easiest way to prevent this waste and save some money is by packing your own lunch and snacks. I bring a lunch bag that holds breakfast, lunch, snacks, and personal items like my wallet and phone. When I plan lunch for the week, I roughly abide by the rule of two salads, two sandwiches, and one leftover. Occasionally, I'll really mix things up with some soup and a side salad.

> **Time-saving tip! Double your batch of soup and freeze it in 16-ounce mason jars. If I'm ever in a huge hurry, I can grab one of those jars out of the freezer. It will be thawed enough to pop in the microwave by lunch.**

The Tools
Snapware (or another glass container), metal tiffins, mason jars of different sizes, and cloth napkins

My Favorite Work Meals
Breakfast:
- Overnight oats (mason jar)
- Chia seed pudding (mason jar)
- Smoothie (mason jar)

- Fresh fruit
- Homemade granola and yogurt (mason jar)
- Pastry (tiffin or cloth napkin)
- Blueberry muffins (tiffin or cloth napkin)
- Banana nut bread (tiffin or cloth napkin)

Salads:
- Taco salad (layered in a mason jar)
- Caesar Salad (layered in a mason jar)
- Green Salad (layered in a mason jar)

I like to carry the salad and toppings in a 32-ounce mason jar and the dressing in a smaller 4-ounce jar. I don't like eating out of the jar. It's hard to get everything equally dispersed, so I move it to a plate or a bowl.

Soup:
- Tomato soup
- Roasted red pepper soup
- Chickpea and dumplings
- Broccoli and cheese
- Butternut squash
- Lentil veggie

I keep my soups in a 16-ounce mason jar for easy transit.

Sandwiches:
- Peanut butter and jelly
- Roasted veggie po' boy
- Meatlessball subs

I could live off sandwiches. There are infinite combinations between two pieces of bread. I pack my sandwiches in metal tiffins.

Sides and Snacks:
- Seasonal fruit: oranges, apples, berries, or a lonely banana
- Bulk snacks like pretzels or granola
- Homemade trail mix
- Chocolate chip cookies
- Veggie sticks and homemade hummus
- Dried fruit
- Energy bites

I typically pack two sides every day and carry snacks in one of the tiffin tiers or in a mason jar. I keep most of these items on hand at home as they have a 1- to 2-week shelf life in the fridge.

> **Lonely bananas are bananas without bunches or mates. Unless you live in native banana land, bananas have a hefty carbon footprint. To combat this, buy the lonely ones. They are typically thrown out at the end of the night by grocers. So if you love bananas, grab all the lonely ones!**

74. Take Out

Just because you're trying to reduce your waste doesn't mean that you can't grab some tasty takeout and bring it back to eat.

If I'm trying a new place, I like to call ahead. It's easy to thoroughly explain to them *what* and *why* I'm making an unusual request. I have a 98-percent success rate of getting food to go in my own container. Calling ahead can save you some time on the off chance the answer is no, and you're in a rush.

I try to avoid going to a new place during peak business hours, when an establishment may not be as accommodating simply because there's so much going on. I typically take my lunch around 1:30 because it's when I'm naturally hungry. It also means most of the restaurants are slowing down.

If someone seems super confused by your request, you can also order your food to stay. Once you get your food, pack it in a to-go container and leave. I try to avoid doing this because I hate dirtying up extra dishes even if I'm not the one washing them. But, sometimes it's the only way.

Tipping well and being polite helps, too! You'd be amazed at how happy they'll be to see you come back with your own containers.

Some people have had luck using their own containers in fast-food chains like Nations and Chipotle, but on average most national chains are less accommodating. I always have success at small family businesses. They're normally really happy to help you with your request because they're more conscious of the fact that to-go containers cost money. It's also nice to support a local business in your community. You can develop a relationship with the owners, and small business owners really care about you as their customer. They are generally very invested in what happens in town, and building this relationship can lead to opportunities to help raise awareness about waste reduction with all of their customers. At a large chain, there can be more of a disconnect, as they report to a corporate headquarters and have less control over decision-making.

The best piece of advice I can give you is to play the part! You have to be confident. Don't ask for something to go in your container. You don't need permission. Politely tell them, with a smile. For example: "Hello, I would like that sandwich to go in this tiffin." *smile* "Thank you." I have yet to be turned down. Having confidence and politely telling them (see how I keep emphasizing *politely?*) alters the power dynamic. When you ask a question, you hand them all of the power. When you *tell* them, you hold onto it. Your confidence will make them believe this is the most normal thing in the world. If someone looks confused or feels awkward about it, I say, "I do this all the time," like it's no big deal . . . because it's not. I really do this all the time. Articulating that tends to ease their worries.

I hope this is a given, but make sure that your containers are appropriately sized and clean. Don't bring a dirty container. They aren't going to wash it for you, and you don't want to make a bad impression.

75. Out to Eat

If you're dining in a nice restaurant, you'll likely encounter "real everything" in terms of dishes, glassware, and flatware. I honestly can't imagine going out to eat at a nice restaurant and being given a paper plate, can you? When visiting dives, though, it can be hit or miss on the disposables.

The first thing I do when going to a new restaurant is to scope out the place online to see how they serve their food. Does it come on real plates? Do they use cloth napkins? Do you see straws in people's drinks? Looking for these kinds of signs ahead of time will help you prevent waste. You can come prepared with a reusable straw or be prepared to ask for your drink without one.

I don't worry too much about paper napkins—I just bring them home to compost. I also bring a small metal tiffin with me in case I have leftovers I need to bring home.

If you're going to a dive with all disposables, you could always bring your own plate. I bring my own plate to the café across from where I work, and they love it! I just bring the plate back and wash it in the sink at work.

Some restaurants have real plates and cups, but serve specialty cold drinks in disposables. It's always so odd to see, but if that's the case, I just ask for my drink to be in a real cup instead of a disposable one. They're typically happy to oblige. It just takes a little bit of courage and bravery to ask.

CHAPTER SEVEN

TRAVEL AND TRANSPORTATION

Traveling can throw a huge wrench in zero-waste efforts. It's difficult to leave behind the routines you've built. As a reminder, zero waste doesn't mean zero emissions, but I'll be covering other ways to lessen your impact beyond just the trash created when traveling.

76. Walk, Bike, Carpool, Take Public Transit

I have a 30-minute rule. If it's under a 30-minute walk, I walk. Of course, I don't always plan well enough, but I find that it's a really good rule of thumb to keep in the back of your mind.

Biking is another great option too. A 30-minute walk is only a 10-minute bike ride. Try to increase the amount of time you spend walking or biking, especially for shorter distances. Shorter trips in the car release more emissions because of all the stop-and-go.

This practice is better for the environment, but also great for your health. Working in an office, I sit at my desk too much. Keeping the 30-minute rule is a nice way to get moving and infuse more exercise into my daily routine.

I live in a small town near the downtown area. It is fairly walkable and bikeable. If you live in a suburb, this might not work for you. Back home in Arkansas, the closest thing to us was a gas station four miles away. Driving was the only choice, but if you do live near a grocery store, corner store, a restaurant, or really any establishment, you frequent try to abide by the 30-minute rule.

I always carpool to the office. Two other employees live near me, and we ride together. Occasionally, if one of us has an appointment or needs to leave work early, we'll go separately, but generally, we find this is a great way to save on gas money. See if anyone you work with lives near you. Or as one of your green office initiatives from Tip 72, you could set up a carpool sheet. People could sign up based on where they live to reduce emissions.

Start a carpool sheet for any hobby activities like group sports or rehearsals. It's always more fun to ride with friends to practice than to drive by yourself. Depending on how many of you are riding, you might even qualify to drive in the carpool lane. You'll be saving money, saving emissions, and saving time.

Fewer cars on the road also means less traffic. Think about how much easier it would be to drive if suddenly the volume of all of the cars on the freeway dropped by a third. You'd be cruising and saving. The constant breaking and accelerating of stop-and-go traffic burns more gas and pumps more pollutants into the air than just driving a steady 65.

You can also consider grabbing public transit. We have a plethora of options in the Bay Area: ferries, trains, and buses, and if you live here, one of them is bound to be going your direction. Check the options and schedules wherever you live—many US cities offer bus service—and try to grab public transit when you can.

77. Zero-Waste Travel Kit

The Boy Scout motto and the zero-waste motto are one in the same: "Be prepared!" But it can be difficult to be prepared when you have no idea where the open road will take you. I am not the kind of person to plan out every single step of a vacation. I like to see where the vacation takes me.

I want to prevent waste, but I also don't want to carry a whole bunch of stuff with me "just in case," because that could get really heavy. What follows is a list of what my husband Justin and I pack in our suitcases—depending on the day or what we're doing we might take some of it with us or just leave it in the hotel room.

Two Insulated Water Bottles

We always have insulated water bottles on us, so we never have to worry about getting thirsty and needing to buy a plastic one. Since they're insulated, we can also grab a hot coffee if we're in a rush, but typically on vacation, we sip it in the café and enjoy our time together.

Depending on our plans for the day, we might only bring one bottle and share. Neither of us likes to be bogged down with a lot of stuff when we travel.

Four Cloth Napkins

I tend to pack two cloth napkins for each of us. They're small and take up very little room. They're also super handy to have around. A cloth napkin is great for drying your hands in a public restroom, blowing your nose, or tying up on-the-go treats like donuts or pastries. Just not in that order . . .

The only downside is that if a cloth napkin gets too soiled, it's not super convenient to wash it. You can always use the hotel sink, though; just make sure you have time for it to dry.

Two Bamboo Cutlery Sets

Justin and I each have a bamboo cutlery set. We don't use them too often, but it's nice to throw in your bag if you think you're going to encounter plastic silverware. Using bamboo won't alert TSA if you're flying, and they're light enough to not make too much of a difference to the weight of your luggage.

Two Tiffins

Justin and I each have a tiffin. I find traveling with two tiffins makes life much easier. I have a nesting set of tiffins that's very convenient to travel with.

When we're traveling, we don't always have time to prep food beforehand. If we each have our own tiffin, we can get sandwiches or donuts placed in our own containers. When we went on our honeymoon, we got sandwiches to go in our tiffins at the airport, so we didn't have to rely on packaged snacks. However, we tend to only carry one tiffin with us, for leftovers at restaurants or snacks when we arrive at our destination.

One Reusable Bag

I typically only bring one reusable bag that folds up really small. We don't shop much on vacation, but I carry it just in case. I might throw in some reusable produce bags if I know we'll be staying for a while and cooking meals in a kitchen.

Dish Soap

Make sure to bring a small bottle of dish soap. This way you can wash your reusable containers in the hotel. I like to travel with Dr. Bronner's because it can be used for everything!

Need to wash some socks or soiled napkins? Dr. B.

Need to wash your body? Dr. B.

Need to wash your dishes? Dr. B.

It's a great multi-tasking item to bring.

78. Zero Waste at Airports

Flying and zero waste in the same sentence is kind of an oxymoron. However, that doesn't mean we can't take strides to make it less wasteful. Several airlines are working to cut emissions by using biofuels. In fact, the Solar Impulse 2, a solar-powered aircraft, successfully flew from Nagoya, Japan to Hawaii in April of 2016.

Changes are happening, but they're happening slowly. For now, we should try to limit our emissions and reduce the amount we fly, because telling people to stop traveling or visiting their family is just not viable. Traveling and getting outside of your normal routine is really important for developing a well-rounded personality. It's important to experience other cultures to grow your worldview. Instead of skipping travel, let's focus on doing it less and traveling better.

Travel Less

Opt for fewer trips for longer periods of time instead of frequent shorter trips. Depending on the distance and the number of people traveling, you may create fewer emissions if you drive.

Five-Hour Rule: The sweet spot for flying while considering how to lower your emissions expense is around 4 to 5 hours. Emissions increase on longer flights due to the weight of the additional fuel the plane must carry. On shorter flights, a higher proportion of the fuel is used taking off and taxiing.

Sit In Economy

Flying in business class results in 3 times more emissions per person.

An Empty Water Bottle

Empty is the very key word here. DO NOT bring a bottle full of water through security. You will get stopped. You will be unable to pour your water down a drain. You will have to choose between chugging it or throwing the water in a trash can.

Sticking to your zero-waste principles, you'll obviously have to chug it. Then you'll have to go through security again. Worst-case scenario, TSA will tease you. You will be late for your flight. This will result in a middle seat, and you will have to pee the whole way.

All of this can be avoided if you just bring an **empty** water bottle.

After you're through security, you can fill your empty water bottle. There should be water fountains by the bathrooms. If not, just pop into a café, and they can fill it up at their soda fountain.

Bring a Snack or Three

You can bring your own food to an airport. I don't know what is it about flying, but it makes me hungry. I can go three hours without a snack on a normal day. But, for some reason, when I'm on a plane, I need my snacks. So, pack your own snack based on the amount time you'll be gone and your hunger level. I bring a small mason jar full of dried blueberries and nuts. I keep the blueberries and nuts in separate mason jars, in case someone on my flight has a nut allergy (passengers with serious allergies will often alert the flight crew who will make an announcement to alert the other passengers). I wouldn't want to put anyone in danger.

Quart-Sized Liquid Bags

You can buy a TSA-approved reusable, quart-sized, clear bag with a zipper. They're sold online and in most stores with a pharmacy section. They typically come with three or four 3-ounce bottles. Fill these with the products you already have. No need to buy travel-sized bottles! I have had my TSA-approved bag-and-bottle set since I was in high school. If you take good care of it, it should last you for many years to come.

Entertainment

I try to hit the library to grab a new book before I go on a trip. Checking a book out from the library is a great way to utilize the sharing economy. Most libraries have digital collections, too, so you can check out e-books and load them onto your phone or e-reader.

79. Zero Waste on the Road

Bring a Cooler

The cooler is your friend. Maybe it's not just airline snacks...
maybe there's just something about traveling that makes me
want to eat.

I have many fond memories of going on road trips with my
parents and being allowed to pick out an unhealthy snack, and
I still get that urge with every road trip I take. The unhealthy
snacks call to me like a siren from within the gas station, luring
me to buy junk food. Of course, junk food isn't very good for you,
and it comes with a lot of unnecessary waste, but it's tempting
nonetheless. I combat the junk food sirens' calls by keeping a
cooler in the car full of tasty and package free snacks. Here are
some of my favorites:

- Bananas
- Apples
- Peanut butter
- Bread
- Hummus
- Veggie sticks
- Jelly

Carrot sticks dipped in hummus and apple slices with peanut
butter are both filling snacks, but if I'm really hungry, I'll make
a PB&J.

Here are a few snacks that can easily be purchased from bulk
bins and don't need refrigeration:

- Roasted chickpeas
- Nuts
- Granola

Real Food

Man cannot live on snacks alone.

Sometimes, all you want is a delicious hot meal. When you're on the road, the choices might be limited to fast food, fast food, and more fast food. Which means packaging, junk, and more packaging.

Look for a sit-down restaurant, like a diner. Diners tend to be open late and serve food on real plates. If you can't find a diner or other sit-down establishment, my favorite fast-food restaurant is Subway. I've eaten there a couple of times since I started my zero-waste journey. Did you know their paper sandwich wraps even says, "Please Compost"? Just make sure you ask for the sandwich without the plastic bag.

If you can't find a Subway, gas stations tend to have self-serve areas with taquitos, samosas, tamales, empanadas, or other foods in display cases. You can easily grab these foods with tongs and place them in your own containers.

If you do wind up at another fast-food place, look for items that come in paper, like burritos from Taco Bell or a hamburger or veggie burger from Burger King. The paper can be composted.

The best way to avoid unwanted plastic waste is to carry your own cup. Most fast-food restaurants are stringently against bringing your own container for food. (Not all are—it doesn't hurt to ask!) Drinks are less of a problem, especially if the ounces are clearly marked on your cup. Make a note of the ounces on the paper cups provided by the establishment, and fill up your reusable bottle. Let the cashier know how many ounces can fit in your cup and what size that corresponds to, and everything should be fine! If they say no to you using your own cup, go topless and strawless.

Compost

While you're traveling, you are probably going to wind up with some organic waste, whether it be a banana peel, an apple core, or a Subway wrapper. Keep a small, sealed bin in your car for food or other compostable scraps to add to your compost when you get home. If the bin is going to be sitting in your warm car for a couple of days, make sure it has a tight seal, and maybe put it in the trunk. If all else fails, you can always bury the compost at a rest stop. And be on the lookout for composting options, whether at local farms, garden clubs, grocery stores, or composting bins offered by the city you're visiting.

Zero-Waste Kit

Since you're driving, you don't have as many space restrictions as you do when you're flying. You can keep a pretty decked-out zero-waste kit, like the one from Tip 77, in your car so that you're prepared for all situations.

Toiletries

When you're road tripping, you don't have liquid restrictions like you do when you're flying. At the same time, you probably don't want to lug around an entire bottle of shampoo. I still decant my shampoo and body wash into travel tubes, but carrying the whole bottle is an option if that's what you prefer. I use Plaine Products, and they have aluminum travel sizes that are so cute!

If you forget your soap and shampoo, use the hotel's. Just make sure to bring the leftovers home, so you can use them on your next trip. If you open anything, don't waste it!

Use Technology

Almost everyone has the Internet in their pocket these days. You can use your phone to look up places to compost, search for restaurants with real plates, and even find grocery stores with bulk bins. Take a couple of minutes to browse Google or Yelp to see if you can find any waste-free solutions.

80. Buying Carbon Offsets

We can't talk about traveling without mentioning carbon offsets. You can purchase carbon offsets online to reduce the emissions of carbon dioxide and other greenhouse gases that you make during travel, heating your home, driving your car, flying in a plane, etc. Offsets are a great way to go the extra mile. There are several organizations that offer carbon offsetting. For a small fee, they will plant trees, create sustainable-waste management plants, and install clean energy in developing countries. I recommend you calculate your carbon footprint yearly and buy offsets accordingly.

My carbon footprint last year was around 6,000 pounds. I calculate this with footprintcalculator.org and then offset my footprint with terrapass.com or plant trees through the USDA Forest Service Plant-A-Tree Program. My yearly offset cost was less than $40, so this is a fairly inexpensive option.

81. Zero-Waste Vacations

We've talked a lot about flying, but what about other aspects of vacations, like where to stay and what to do?

Hotels are surprisingly high in carbon emissions. They're responsible for 60 million tons each year! Now, I'm not saying you should never stay in another hotel again, but I am suggesting that you think a little bit outside of the box.

Eco-hotels are becoming more and more popular. There are several certifications you can look for when researching hotels to help you make a good decision. The most popular certifications to look for are EarthCheck, Green Globe, and Sustainable Tourism Eco-Certificate. If you're in the US, you can also check on whether or not your potential hotel is a LEED building or take a look at its Energy Star Rating. There are many other certifications depending on what part of the world you're in, but some of the things you might look for include:

- Energy reduction
- Land stewardship
- Composting
- Solar panels
- Giving back
- Supporting the local community
- Conservation education
- Building materials
- Bike share

Ecotourism has been on the rise in recent years. A lot of areas aren't prepared to receive an influx of tourism, which can threaten local ecosystems and cultures. Ecotourism is focused on creating a positive impact. Its aim is to sustain the livelihood of the local people and conserve the environment. If you visit Belize, you can go to a Community Baboon Sanctuary where citizens have preserved their land to support the endangered monkey. Your tourist dollars go to supporting not only an endangered species but also healthy forests and the ability of locals to more easily look after the land. Some other ecotourism ideas include a trip to help remove non-native plant species, or to volunteer at a local farm to learn about the local climate. You can also always visit a homestead, or pitch a tent and go off grid.

CHAPTER EIGHT

SPECIAL EVENTS

Special events often involve details out of your control, but there are ways to plan ahead and reduce your impact.

82. Keep It Real

When hosting special events, I use real plates, real forks, real cups, and cloth napkins. I always recommend starting the party with an empty washing machine and an empty dishwasher. This way when the end of the night rolls around, you can easily put the linens in the washing machine, the dishes in the dishwasher, press a button, and go to bed.

If you don't have a dishwasher, like me, take up your friends on their offer to help you clean up! My friends are more than happy to help me wash dishes. They stay a little after the party, we drink a little wine, and we all have fun cleaning up.

I have found clean-up to be quicker at parties that have reusables compared to disposables. There's some psychological, deep-rooted respect for real items. People treat them very differently than disposables. If you have disposable cups, plates, and napkins at a party, people will set them down, forget about them, and then get new ones. You might have only invited 40 people over to your party, but you'll go through 60 plates. People will keep track of their glass glasses, ceramic plates, and cloth napkins much better simply because it's real. A lot of people end up not wanting to even grab a cloth napkin and will forgo it, hovering around the snack table instead.

Pro Tip: To remember which glass belongs to whom, write the name of the owner on it with a washable marker or wax pencil.

If you don't have enough dishes or cloth napkins for a party, ask a friend or family member if you can borrow some. The last time we threw a big party, we borrowed a couple of chairs, tables, and some extra cups. People were more than happy to lend a helping hand. Sharing supplies is so much better than having to buy and store them.

83. Decor

The most sustainable decor is decor you already have. The second most sustainable decor is decor that is natural and compostable. Decor that you create from your natural surroundings is beautiful, simple, and will drastically change for each holiday, season, and party—which is half the fun!

I try not to go too overboard with decoration, but I do like to add festive touches. Working with the seasons is super important when picking out your decor. You don't want to buy flowers that have been shipped halfway around the world. If I were throwing a party in December, when there aren't many floral options in season, I would focus on an arrangement made from gorgeous twigs and candles. It's inviting, warm, and plays into the spirit of the season.

A nice sit-down Thanksgiving might have miniature pumpkins used as place settings with a larger pumpkin in the center hollowed out to store a beautiful bouquet of flowers. How amazing would it be for the hollowed-out pumpkin centerpiece to be the same pumpkin that provided the crunchy pumpkins seeds that top the salad? The smaller pumpkins can be turned into soup at a later date, and all of the pumpkin skins can be composted and returned to nature. It's party decor and food with a full life-cycle and zero-waste mindset.

If you're having an Easter brunch, maybe the place settings are naturally dyed hard-boiled eggs, which can be eaten by the guests or saved for lunch later in the week. Maybe the centerpiece of the table is a gorgeous bouquet of in-season flowers. Roses are typically in season in spring. After the roses have started to wilt, you can turn the petals into a beautiful rose water or use them for a floral bath. Afterward, you can compost the stems and remaining petals.

I also like to get creative with my holiday food: a cake in the shape of a rabbit for Easter, an ornate pie for Thanksgiving, even spooky crudités for Halloween—you can turn a cauliflower into a brain or carve a set of carrot fingers to dip into a beet-red hummus. The options are endless. There's no reason you have to turn to cheaply made decor to throw a beautiful party.

And we can't talk about decor without considering ambiance. Ambiance plays a huge part in decoration and setting the mood. So, dim some lights, light some candles, and make sure you have the perfect music to accompany your event.

84. Finger Foods vs. Sit-Down Meals

When moving to a zero-waste lifestyle, you're cutting off most convenience foods. This is great because it's much healthier. However, this can also be tough when you're cooking for a crowd.

When planning a party, I first take a look at the guest list. If I'm having a small gathering, around ten people and under, a sit-down dinner is appropriate and fairly easy to arrange. If I'm having more than ten, the party will have a snack table for people to graze at as the party rages.

The next step is to take the season and weather into consideration. Both the season and the weather will dictate location, menu, and your decorations. For instance, corn is a popular dish for Thanksgiving, but corn isn't in season then. What to do?

This brings us to my favorite part—planning the menu. A week before the party, I take really good stock of what's available at the farmers' market. This is how I start all of my menus. I always check with the farmers to make sure they'll be back the following week, and that what I need will be in season.

I try to make sure I have a mix of prep-ahead food, easy-to-assemble food, and one or two show-stopping dishes. This ensures I'm not spending hours slaving away in the kitchen, and that I'm able to enjoy my party.

The two show-stopping dishes are typically more complex and a little more time-consuming. It's a way for me to have fun, integrate the theme of the party, and infuse some edible decoration. If we were doing a sit-down Thanksgiving dinner, how darling would it be to have mini-pies with everyone's name written in pie crust for place settings? Practical, edible, and show-stopping.

Sit-Down Meal

I keep sit-down meals simple with a starter salad, bread for the table, a main, two sides, and a dessert. I'll buy several bottles of red and white wines, and will make a big batch of tea for those who don't drink. Sit-down meals are more intimate and more uniform, making them easier to plan. Everyone will be eating the same food, so it's easy to find ways to save time.

One of the ways I save time is by buying bread and dessert from a local bakery. I buy the bread in a bread bag and heat the bread up in the oven before everyone comes over. It's so nice and warm. I place it in a basket covered with a cloth napkin just like at the fancy restaurants. And I bring my cake carrier to the bakery and get a cake to go. No one has to know you didn't make these things. Your zero-waste secret is safe with me.

My next tip is to keep your sides *very* simple. There's no need to make complex side dishes. Sometimes, ingredients are better left simple. Let those fresh, tasty veggies from the farmers' market shine. Don't over complicate your life if you don't have to.

Finger Food

Larger parties with food tables full of snacks will make your life more complicated. You have to have multiple options for guests to graze on throughout the night. For each invited guest, a good rule of thumb is to have 12 nibbles and 3 alcoholic or non-alcoholic drinks.

To keep my life easier on the clean-up side, I stick to finger food. Finger food can be eaten with a cloth napkin, so there's no need to wash plates or cutlery at the end of the night. Plus, people will tend to hover around the table, snacking, and avoiding the cloth napkins.

Here's how I break it down:

Two drinks:

1. Alcoholic: I really like to make sangria if the weather is warm, or mulled wine if it's chilly. Both use red wine as the base because for me, living in California near Napa Valley, there is no shortage of red wine. Plus they're tasty, easy crowd pleasers. If there's a popular locally sourced alcoholic beverage made where you are, I suggest you try that!

2. Non-Alcoholic: I usually make lemonade or tea. Tea is much easier to prepare than lemonade, so I go with that option if I'm running short on time.

Five foods that don't need to be prepared:

1. Crudités ALL day. If you come to a party of mine, I can guarantee you will find a smattering of fresh vegetables ready for dipping.

2. Charcuterie board: It's so easy to go to your local deli to stock up on different meats and cheeses.

3. Dips and spreads: I try to have three dips and spreads. I always make a fresh batch of hummus, then I whip up an olive tapenade or an onion jam, and I keep the last one simple with rustic stoneground mustard that I buy in a glass jar.

4. Olives: Delis typically have olives available, so you don't have to rely on the ones in the jar.

5. Nuts: Having a party mix is always popular. You can buy nuts from your local grocery store from bulk bins, toss them in a couple of spices, place them on a baking tray, and toast until

fragrant. I love to toss nuts with a little bit of lime zest, chili powder, salt, and red pepper flakes.

6. Bread: I grab a couple of baguettes from the bakery and slice them into small pieces so people can make small sandwiches if they want to.

Two foods that you make:
The possibilities here are endless. Your choices could be sweet or savory, but you'll want to make sure that they're center stage so everyone can *Ooo* and *Ahh* over your creativity. Some of the things I've made for parties are mini-pies, sliders, pretzel bites, caramel apple dippers, baked ravioli, chicken/veggie nuggets, and taco cups.

Two desserts:
1. Fruit: You want to make sure the fruit is easy to grab and eat. It also needs to be appetizing. I'm not sure anyone would grab a slice of banana—yuck. But, if it's berry season, a gorgeous bowl of strawberries would be easy for people to grab.

2. Cookies or cupcakes: You can bake these or you can pick some up from your bakery. It's easy to prep these ahead of time, and they're finger-food friendly. I bake my cupcakes without liners, so people don't have to worry about what to do with them when they're finished.

Compost and Recycling
When you're throwing a large party, make sure to put out recycling and compost bins and label them clearly. This always helps with cleanup and guests will know where to put their empties and food waste if they have any.

85. Storing and Sending Leftovers

I have several glass baking dishes and mixing bowls that come with lids. They're simple dishes, and I serve all of my party foods in them. At the end of the night, I can put the lid on and go to bed. It makes clean-up an absolute breeze! And if I'm left with more food than I can eat before it goes bad, I send some home with guests.

> *How to send guests home with leftovers ... the zero-waste way:* I still buy things in glass jars at the supermarket like pasta sauce, mustard, salad dressing, and maybe olives. I wash those jars and keep them on hand for when guests come over. You can send home tasty treats without the trash!

86. Forget Party Favors

I don't feel like this tip needs much more elaboration. I've never been to a party and said, "Man, I wish I had a party favor." In fact, I typically try to avoid them at all costs. When hostesses hand me a party favor, I'm the guest that typically "forgets" and "accidentally" sets it down somewhere. Oops. I make a motion to abolish party favors altogether.

87. Hostess Gifts

Now, while I am anti-party favor, I am a firm believer in hostess gifts. If you're going to someone else's home, you should never show up empty-handed. The best hostess gifts are consumable. They can choose to share with guests or save it for themselves for later. These are my four go-to hostess gifts:

- A loaf of freshly baked bread
- Bottle of wine
- Fresh flowers
- A box of nice loose-leaf tea

88. Special Occasion Clothing

Special occasion clothing can be the dress you need for your friend's wedding, a tux for a gala, or a hot-pink, zebra mini-skirt for one of your theatre friends' many themed parties. It's the clothing you wear once or twice and aren't sure if/when you'll wear again . . .

Thrift Shop

When I was a full-time actor, we had a lot of parties, and they were all themed. All of them. We didn't have a single normal party. This meant we wore countless costumes! Some of my favorite parties were the White Trash Bash (where you'd wear the hot-pink, zebra mini-skirt), Superhero vs. Villains, and a Bedsheet Toga Party (where I met my husband!). When dressing for these parties, I consistently wound up purchasing something from the thrift store and then re-donating it after the party. Justin and I would often go thrifting together to find clever costumes for each week's theme.

On average I spent about $5–10 per costume. I just considered it a "rental" fee. You might be surprised what you find at your local thrift store. Even for more formal events, they have a fairly decent selection.

Borrow

Never underestimate your friend's closet. In college, I had a lot of dresses. My boyfriend at the time was in politics, and we attended tons of dinners, fundraisers, and other fancy events. I had over 200 dresses . . . yep, a lot of dresses. Because I had so many, several of my sorority sisters would come over and borrow dresses for our events on campus.

Rent

Renting is a fabulous option if you don't want to wear the same dress to every event. There are several sites online where you can rent dresses for an evening and send them back. It's a great way to wear something super nice for a fraction of the price.

You can also rent tuxes for formal events, although one nice suit will take you far. My husband has one really nice dark gray suit that he wears for everything. He wears it for galas, openings, the theatre, weddings—hell, he even wore it to our wedding! If we're attending a strict black-tie or white-tie event, he rents a proper tuxedo.

> An easy way to dress for a black-tie event without renting or buying a full tuxedo is to buy a tux shirt and wear it with a nice black suit! Use the items you already have to save on resources and save some cash!

Consign

Consignment shops tend to be a little more high-end than thrift stores because they have more control over their inventory. You can find some really, really amazing pieces at a good deal. If you wear it and don't wear it again, you can always re-consign it and recoup some of your cost.

Shop Online

When looking for specific purchases, there's a ton of secondhand options online like thredUP, Poshmark, and eBay. You are buying sight unseen so make sure you ask a lot of questions and know your measurements.

Measure your bust, waist, top of the hip, full hip, inseam, and waist to floor. You should always have those measurements handy when shopping online. Sizes change from designer to designer, but measurements are reliable. If you're shopping online, buy well before your event just in case it doesn't work out. If you love what you bought but it just needs a little bit of an adjustment, take it to your local tailor. They can fit it perfectly to your body so you have a piece that you can wear for years to come.

Buy New

If you can't find anything secondhand, then look at purchasing something new and sustainable. There are a lot of designers who are working to fix both social and environmental problems.

89. Gift Ideas

I divide gifts into three different categories: Consumables, Experiences, and Things. I have absolutely no problem with buying things if the person I'm gifting the thing to really needs or wants it. The problem lies in wandering around a gift shop for an hour and settling on a knick-knack that kind of reminds you of the person. That is the worst way to buy a gift. If you're in that situation, buy a consumable or an experience.

Consumables

I remember, as a kid, loving to open and receive presents. I also remember dreading putting all of my spoils away. My room was always packed with stuff, and I had to reorganize after every holiday to make room for my things. I remember my favorite gifts were gifts that could be consumed. I mean, the chocolate never lasted long enough for me to have to "put it up." I've always been a pretty diehard fan of consumables.

1. Coffee beans
2. Candles
3. Spice mixes
4. Homemade hot cocoa mix
5. Brownie mix
6. Hot sauce
7. Loose-leaf tea
8. Infused vodka
9. Cookie mix
10. Fresh fruit

11. Holiday cookies
12. Nut butter
13. Dry shampoo
14. DIY lotion
15. Body butter
16. Sugar scrub
17. Homemade vinegar
18. Candy from bulk bins in a mason jar
19. Bath salts
20. Lip balm
21. Nice bottle of wine
22. Lotion bar
23. Homemade chocolates
24. Homemade vanilla extract
25. Fudge
26. Growler of beer
27. Nice bottle of liquor
28. Home-cooked meal
29. Candied peels
30. Apple butter
31. Freshly baked bread
32. Jam
33. Flowers
34. Peanut brittle
35. Potpourri
36. Dried herbs
37. Baked goods
38. Crispy chickpeas
39. Solid perfume
40. Salty snack mix

Experience Gifts

Let's face it—when you hear someone say, "Experience gift," you immediately think *expensive*. At least I do. When I hear, "Experience gift," I think vacations, skydiving, tickets to concerts, and sporting events, but experience gifts don't have to be expensive. I've broken these experience gifts down by price point, to help you gift experiences.

When you give an experience gift to a friend, make sure to offer them at least three dates for them to claim their prize. If you don't, you put too much pressure on the receiver to make the plan, and it can come off like an empty gift. You might also want to consider making a card or a little coupon/ticket to give to the receiver (assuming their experience doesn't come with one), so they have a physical reminder.

$ Experience Gifts (Under $30)

1. Coffee: The gift of coffee is a great one. I love to take my friends out for a cup of joe or a nice cup of tea so we can spend an hour catching up.

2. Ice cream: A trip to the ice-cream parlor is another simple gift. Go with a friend to grab a cone of your favorite flavor—mine is vegan chocolate peanut butter! Place it in a sugar cone to keep it zero waste.

3. Hike: Grab a friend for an afternoon, pack some homemade granola, and get out in nature. Spend some time soaking up the beautiful scenery and good conversation.

4. Picnic: Head to a park for the afternoon and enjoy some tasty homemade treats. Just remember to keep it zero waste by packing your treats in reusables, or grab takeout like in Tip 74.

5. Ice skating: I always loved ice skating, especially in the winter. Grab your favorite scarf, mittens, and BFF for a fun trip to the rink! Grab some hot cocoa with extra marshmallows, too—just remember to get it in a real mug.

6. Roller skating: Roller rinks were the hit birthday-party activity when I was growing up. Throw it back with your friends and rent some rollerblades, or break yours out from a couple of years ago.

7. Go out for a drink: Invite your friend out to the bar for a drink. Even better, go on the weekly trivia night for some extra fun.

8. Gardening/composting class: Many local community gardens offer composting and gardening workshops. How fun would it be to learn a new skill with your friend.

9. Movie tickets for two: Catch one of the latest flicks with your friend. You can grab some candy in bulk and sneak in it in your bag or just pick out candies that come in a cardboard box like Dots or Raisinettes. Compost the box when you're done!

10. Bowling: Bowling night is a blast! I love bowling with friends, and the alley we go to even serves pints of beer in real glasses, woot-woot! Treat your friend to a fun night of strikes and spares.

11. Lecture: It's always nice to attend a lecture on a topic you're interested in. When Justin and I first moved to California, we got each other tickets to a lecture at the California Academy of the Sciences for Valentine's Day.

12. Comedy or improv show for two: There are a lot of comedy and improv shows done by local troupes. Check one out for a night of laughs.

13. Arcade: Pizza and pinball—I can't think of a more fun night!

Challenge your friend to all of the arcade games, like Mrs. PacMan, Twin Racer, and the King of Fighters.

14. Batting cages or driving range: On that same page, a lot of arcades have batting cages, driving ranges, or go-karts. There are many fun ways to spend time with your friends that don't involve walking around the mall.

$$ Experience Gifts (Under $60)

15. A foraging trip for two: My friend took one of these local foraging hikes, and it sounded like so much fun! Get outside and learn about the local flora and fauna.

16. Laser tag or mini-golf: Mini-golf and laser tag are such fun events! Head out with a friend or two for a wildly competitive evening.

17. Rock climbing: It's nice to center friend activities around being active since so many of our activities with others are normally food-based.

18. Fermentation workshop for two: Fermentation workshops are all the rage right now, and the perfect way to learn a new skill with your friend.

19. Two museum tickets: Justin and I are definitely museum people. Get two tickets and take a friend to a new exhibit that just opened. Also, consider a yearly pass to a Children's Museum for a young nephew, niece, son, daughter, or other young relatives—they'll make months of memories!

20. Campground for a weekend: Plan a camping weekend with a friend. You can typically rent a local campground site inexpensively. Don't forget a cooler full of zero-waste snacks!

21. Pub crawl: A pub crawl typically involves going to two or three breweries and trying a flight of beer at each one.

22. Trampoline place for two: Get your bounce on! Trampoline parks look like so much fun.

23. Escape room: Escape rooms are my favorite! Spend an hour solving puzzles and try to escape!

24. Yoga passes for a month: If your friend is a total yogi, buy them passes to their favorite yoga studio for a gift that keeps giving all month long.

25. Chocolate workshop: Wouldn't it be so fun to go learn how to make delicious chocolates with your bestie? Then you could come home, watch a movie, and eat all of your spoils! Sounds like a perfect day to me.

26. Theatre show: There are always shows going on, so grab tickets to a musical or play and support your local theatre scene. You can grab a drink at a bar afterward and discuss all of your favorite moments.

27. Tickets to a minor-league or college sporting event: Minor-league games or college games tend to cost less than the pro games, but are still just as fun. I used to go see the Arkansas Travelers, our local minor-league baseball team, play all the time. It was a lot of fun to hang out at those games with friends.

28. Wine tasting: Wine tasting is one of my favorite activities when friends and family come to visit in California, and I always joke that it's my favorite zero-waste activity. You're drinking very local to the source, wineries tend to be very low waste as everything is compostable, and you get to enjoy the drink in a glass—so, no disposables.

29. Dance lessons: Take your sweetie out for a tango, salsa, or swing class! Spend the night twirling away.

30. Bathhouse for two: Spend the day in a bathhouse for a luxu-

rious present. Steam rooms, hot tubs, and pools provide such a relaxing atmosphere.

31. Sponsor a run: Have a friend that loves to run? Races cost money, so why not sponsor them for a run? Even better, buy a slot for you, too, and get yourself an exercise buddy.

32. Zip lining: A couple of years back I went zip lining in the Ozarks. It was SO MUCH FUN! A great experience gift for a friend or family member.

$$$ Experience Gifts (Under $150)

33. Massage: Who doesn't love the gift of pampering? This is my mom's favorite gift, and I've gifted Justin a couples massage, too. (Of course, that's kind of like a double gift.)

34. Facial: A facial is another great way to pamper someone you love.

35. Dinner: It's always nice to take your friend out to a nice dinner or gift them a gift card to their favorite restaurant. Giving someone a break from cooking and a chance to indulge in a couple of drinks, an app, an entrée, and a dessert to share is a real treat.

36. Bread-making class: I've seen a couple of bread-making classes advertised recently that look like so much fun! Giving the gift of making bread is a gift that keeps on giving.

37. Musical classes for a month: Has your friend or loved one wanted to learn how to play a musical instrument? Buy them a month of classes!

38. Cooking class: Take a class with a friend or loved one and learn how to make a new cuisine. You can take your new skills and host a party for friends and family.

39. Tandem skydiving: If you're looking for an adventurous time

for you and a pal, nothing says "I love life!" like jumping out of a plane together.

40. Opera tickets: Opera costs a little more than musicals or plays, but it's a wonderful time! Justin got me tickets to the opera for my birthday.

41. Theme park passes: Season passes to a local theme park are a great way to have fun when the weather's nice.

42. Sailing trip: If you live by the water, there are lots of boats you can charter for sunset cruises. Take a loved one out on the water for a memorable 1- to 2-hour long trip.

$$$$ Experience Gifts ($200 and Up)

43. Hot-air balloon: I've always wanted to ride in a hot air balloon. It sounds so lovely!

44. Concert tickets: Snag a pair of tickets to see your loved one's favorite artist.

45. Tickets to a major sporting event: If your friends or family members are big sports fans, tickets to see their team play is a great gift! I always get tickets for Justin to see the Celtics play.

46. Cycling ride tour for two: Grab a pal and get ready to hit the open road. Here in wine country, there are a ton of guided bike tours that include lunch and wine tasting. Find out what's available in your area!

47. Photo shoot: Hire a photographer to take family photos.

48. Chef's tasting menu: I have always wanted to sit down and experience a chef's tasting menu—what a lovely way to spend an evening.

49. Gym membership: This gift will keep giving all year round.

50. Trip: You could also get really extravagant and buy someone a

trip! Someday, I know that I will surprise Justin with a weekend trip to Boston to see his beloved Celtics play at home.

Receiving Gifts

I always encourage everyone to make a list ahead of gift-giving celebrations. By making a list, you can navigate presents. You can make sure you're getting something you want and something that adds value to your life. For my birthday last year, I got a dish rack, an external hard drive, and tickets to the harvest ball at one of the wineries in Napa. So, two things I really needed, and a fun experience, too!

When making your list, think about experiences, consumables that you like, or things that you really need. Most importantly, send the list early for those who plan in advance. In my family, Christmas lists have to be sent no later than July.

I like to add notes to my wish list. This way I can explain why I want a gift and emphasize how it fits into my values. This is the place to talk about fair-trade, made in America/responsibly, warranties, plastic, and trash. For example, the dish rack I got had a note next to it saying, "I like that it's mostly stainless steel and that it has a five-year warranty." By making notes, there becomes a very obvious pattern. Whether I'm offering information about craftsmanship, warranties, or end-of-life options, I'm painting a broader picture to help my family understand what I want. This will also help them if they decide to deviate from the list.

If you haven't already spoken with your family about wanting to live a zero-waste life, you should. You can't be upset about a gift you receive if you haven't been clear with your family about your values. No one wants to buy you a bad present! So, you need to condition them to what a good present means to you, and the time to have that conversation is before they give you a gift, not while you're opening it.

Even after you explain things to your family, they're not always going to do things according to your plan. Sometimes people aren't going to stick to the list. Just roll with it and be kind. I know some people that will flat out reject a gift, but I don't think that's appropriate. I wouldn't do that. I would accept the gift and sincerely thank them. Then, at a *much* later date, talk about it openly and kindly.

You should ask for gifts with no packing peanuts, or gifts with less plastic wrap, or gifts without wrapping paper, but DO NOT have that conversation while you're opening a gift. That is a recipe for disaster, and someone's feelings will get hurt. The gift-giver is trying to do something nice. They are not trying to ruin your day.

A gift is meant to be received, but a gift does not have to be kept. After you receive the gift, it is up to you what you do with it. You can donate it, sell it, or use it. Do not let sentimentality bind you to a gift you aren't crazy about. For more information see Tip 64.

$90.$ Gift Wrapping

Does your grandma fold every piece of wrapping paper? Save every bag and every shred of tissue? That's good. Be like grandma!

When you don't have tons of leftover wrappings to reuse, check out these zero-waste ideas.

Wrapping

- Shopping bags: I always find shopping bags in the recycling bin at work. If the bag has a brand logo on it, you can always cover it with a greeting card.
- Butcher paper: With the amount of online shopping people do in my office, there's never a short supply of butcher paper in the recycle bins. You can always doodle festive drawings on the paper, or keep it plain and add some pizzazz in other ways.
- Newsprint: I think newsprint is such a cute wrapping idea.
- Silk scarves: Of course, they don't have to be real silk, but there's always a plethora of these scarves at the thrift store. They make such a beautiful addition to any present and are a present in themselves.
- Cloth napkins: Cloth napkins are a little more rigid than silk scarves, but I tie them both the same way. The knot on top makes a cute bow. Cloth napkins are also a dime a dozen at the thrift store. They come in all different colors, perfect for any scheme to go with your additional decorations.

Additional Decorations

This is where you get to be really creative! I love designing packages. Some of my favorite decorations are listed below:

- Twine: When I tie a present in brown paper or newsprint, much like in the *Sound of Music*, I tie my packages up with string. I've had a spool of cotton string in the house for years. It can be used to make homemade candles, to truss poultry or make a bouquet garni, or to tie up packages.

- Broaches: I love broaches. I used to have a whole bunch back home. There are so many beautiful ones in thrift stores or maybe in your grandmother's jewelry box. When you tie your packages up with scarves or napkins, pin them on the bow to add a little bit of festivity.

- Bracelets: Bracelets also make a great addition to cloth napkins. Tie the bracelet around the knot to add a little bit of extra sparkle.

- Dried oranges: Dried oranges are some of my favorite holiday decorations. They smell amazing and are SO easy to make. I thinly slice the oranges and sandwich them between a cloth tea towel, and set them on a metal drying rack for 24 hours. Then I bake them on the drying rack for 2 to 3 hours at 200 degrees Fahrenheit. Leftover dried oranges can be boiled with cinnamon sticks to make a stove-top potpourri.

- Cinnamon sticks: Another beautiful and compostable decoration! Tie them with some string and add a splash of greenery for a beautiful present.

- Fresh herbs: I'm biased toward rosemary because it's the only type of herb I have managed not to kill in my garden. It's also hearty and festive so it will stay green on your packages instead of turning brown.

- Bolo ties: I spent a good portion of my childhood in San

Antonio, Texas. I have several bolo ties, and I think they make some very festive decorations for presents.

- Old Christmas cards: For years, I have collected old Christmas cards. I cut the signature portion off and leave the front with the pretty pictures to add to packages and use in the future.
- Pine needles: The fresh scent of pine is lovely and oh-so festive! Nothing says happy holidays more than a couple of festive pine needles. You can typically go pick up some fallen branches for free from the local Christmas tree lot. Since I don't have a tree, I plan on grabbing some branches to put in a vase as a mini-tree for our tiny house.

CHAPTER NINE

ZERO WASTE AND BEYOND

Once you master the simple swaps and find your perfect zero-waste routine, it's time to spread the word. Get involved with your community. Teach others a new skill. Band together to influence local businesses and policy. Together we can change the world.

91. Zero-Waste Pets

When it comes to pets, one of the best things you can do is adopt! Justin and I adopted our dog when she was one year old, and it was one of the best decisions we've ever made.

Zero-Waste Dogs

FOOD:

When buying dog food, you have a couple of options:

- Check with your local co-op. They frequently have dog food available to purchase in bulk.
- Check with a local feed supply store, which may have a whole bunch of different types of pet food in bulk, and treats too!
- Buy dog food in recyclable packaging. I buy my food from Open Farm because they have partnered with TerraCycle and are focused on sustainability.

I don't recommend making your own dog food. I did a lot of research on this because I thought I could handle it, but the vitamins and minerals dogs need are very different from human nutritional requirements. In one study, 100 vets were asked to come up with a meal plan to meet a dog's nutritional needs, and only seven plans provided contained complete nutrition.

TREATS:

If you have a dog boutique in town, they probably have a treat bar where you can fill up on treats in your own cloth bags. Of course, you can always make your own dog treats or opt for some of my favorite package free options:

- apple slices
- carrot slices
- tortilla chips

Occasionally, I also buy a can of wet dog food and put a spoonful into her dry food as a treat. Just remember to rinse and recycle the can.

TOYS:
Appropriate toys are very specific to your own dog. I know that my dog, Nala (a 50-pound husky), will destroy a stuffed animal in three seconds flat, so we don't buy any stuffed or squeaky toys anymore. If your dog likes stuffed animals, you can now purchase really cute ones made from compostable fabric like hemp.

I like to buy longer-lasting toys like bones. Nala loves antlers and Himalayan Dog Chews. We pick up a new one every couple of months, and I've found both sold with minimal packaging at the pet store. When the antlers get too small for Nala to safely chew, I pass them along to a friend's smaller dog.

POOP:
Please pick up after your dog. Currently, there is no zero-waste solution for dog poop. You can only compost dog poop in your own backyard or with a special dog poop composting program. There aren't many areas with dog poop composting programs at this time but check in your area for availability.

I let Nala go in our backyard before we go out for a walk and then I shovel the poop into a separate compost bin, which significantly cuts down on the usage of dog bags.

- Bio Bags are certified compostable, and although you can't compost them in a normal industrial facility, you are still supporting a plastic-free future by opting for plastic-free doggie bags.
- Flushpuppies is another plastic-free option. They are made of a polyvinyl alcohol that the company claims is certified compostable and dissolvable in water; any remaining pieces that have not dissolved will be filtered out by the water processing plant, like toilet paper. I called my local water plant to confirm that was true and to get their opinion; they didn't know.
- Toilet paper is another plastic-free option. Bring toilet paper on your walk and then flush it at home. This may or may not be practical for you, depending on the size of your dog and the length of your walks.

Zero-Waste Cats

FOOD:

All the same options for zero- or low-waste cat food are available for cats that are available for dogs, plus you can also look for wet food packaged in recyclable (plastic-free) cans.

TREATS:

My local pet boutique carries cat treats in bulk. In addition, here are a couple of great treats you could easily keep on hand for a cat:

- frozen blueberries
- frozen banana slices
- steamed carrot slices
- small, steamed florets of broccoli
- slices of cucumber

You could also grab a small spoonful of wet food or wet treats that come in a can. Just remember to rinse and recycle the can.

TOYS:
Cats don't need a ton of fancy toys to keep themselves entertained. Try a few of these easy DIY options:
- Tie a feather to a stick
- Tie or sew up some catnip in an old sock
- Make a scratch post with a 2-by-4 board and some jute rope
- Cut a few holes in a cardboard box

POOP:
This is where things get a little tricky. First of all, make sure you're opting for biodegradable cat litter. Some of the natural alternatives to clay are made from walnuts, cedar, recycled newsprint, and wheat.

There's quite the debate over flushing cat poop. On the don't flush side: toxoplasmosis, a parasite found in cat feces, can infect and kill marine animals like sea otters; toxoplasmosis can't be destroyed by normal sewage treatments.

On the flush side: cats can only spread toxoplasmosis for a few weeks after they've been infected with the microscopic parasite called *Toxoplasma gondii*. Symptoms rarely appear in cats so it can be difficult to tell if they have the parasite. The only way for cats to be exposed to the parasite is by killing and eating raw prey that is infected with toxoplasmosis or through another infected cat's feces. If you have an indoor cat that only eats cooked meat or store-bought food, the chances that your cat is exposed to the toxoplasma parasite is very low. If you do decide to flush your cat poop, then get your cat tested to make sure they're in the clear.

When I was growing up, my mom had a cat named Zack who pooped straight into the toilet. If you go the toilet training route, you get rid of the need for a litter box altogether. (Just make sure your cat is toxoplasma free!)

92. Zero-Waste Guide to Moving

I have moved a lot. My dad was in the Air Force; I am a professional actor. Neither of those jobs allows you to stay in one place for very long. No matter how many times you move, it doesn't get any more enjoyable, but I feel like I have it almost down to a science.

If you were struggling with getting rid of things in chapter 5, just try moving. You will begin to question every purchase you've ever made. Minimizing certainly helps with moving because the fewer possessions you have, the faster moving becomes. Since I move so often most of my stuff is organized with moving in mind.

I store a lot of my belongings in organizational bins, which act as their own moving boxes. Even if you don't move often, you can implement this trick. Many things work as their own moving "boxes," like Rubbermaid tubs, drawers, bags, suitcases, even the laundry hamper. Instead of opting for bubble wrap, I wrap my dishes in cloth napkins or cloth produce bags. I'll slip cups into socks and wrap china in towels.

You will still probably need a few more boxes, so search for moving boxes on Craigslist. I'm sure there will be several free boxes for you to pick-up. After you move, re-list them to help someone else out! When looking for boxes, you can also check grocery stores and liquor stores. Liquor stores have boxes with built-in dividers, which are great for glasses!

93. Disaster Preparedness

I think it's really important to have a disaster kit. It doesn't have to be extravagant, but a few simple things like a first-aid kit, bottled water, canned food, some extra clothes, a flashlight, batteries, a radio, pet food, medication, and whatever else you need could be very helpful if a disaster struck.

Yes, I have plastic bottles of water in my earthquake kit. *gasp* Not every part of your life is going to be zero waste, and that's OK. We don't live in a perfect circular economy. We live in a linear economy, and you have to do what's best for you and your family. Putting your health or safety in jeopardy in the name of wanting to reduce trash is silly.

94. Zero-Waste Burial

I used to joke that the only way to truly be zero waste was to die, but after planning a funeral, I realized you *can* be pretty wasteful even in death.

My grandmother passed away last year. She was my hero, and it was really hard on me. My mother and I both planned the funeral arrangements, and we looked into eco-friendly alternatives. My grandmother hated funerals. She wouldn't have been very pleased with an open casket and a big hurrah.

Traditional burials aren't environmentally friendly. Bodies are pumped full of formaldehyde to preserve them, the coffins don't break down, they're often locked inside of a cement vault underground, and the top is just grass. Grass requires a lot of water and maintenance and provides little to no value. Cremation isn't much better, though. It releases a lot of toxins into the air, but we decided it was more eco-friendly than the standard burial process. The most eco-friendly method is liquid cremation, using only a quarter of the carbon used in traditional cremation, but it's only legal in eight states.

We held a small party for my grandmother at our home in Arkansas. We planted her ashes in a compostable urn to nurture the soil at the base of a baby willow tree, but here are a few of the other options we discovered. Some of them are a little out there, but no matter—make sure you talk to your loved ones about how you want your funeral and remains to be handled.

Pine Box

You can also just keep it really simple with no embalming, no fancy box, and no concrete vault. Using a plain pine box and forgoing the embalming process will allow your body to naturally return to the earth.

Mushroom Suit

With the mushroom suit, you can forgo the box altogether. The suit is made of organic cotton and is infused with a bio mix that contains mushrooms and other microorganisms, which aid in decomposition. They help neutralize toxins in the body and transfer nutrients to plant life.

Tree Urns

Several companies offer tree urns. Most place a portion of the ashes inside of a fully biodegradable container. The container holds a tree seed and uses the nutrients of the remains to grow. I think it would be lovely to have forests memorializing our loved ones instead of our current cemeteries.

Reef Ball

The ashes of your loved one are mixed with concrete to create a reef ball. Reef balls are placed in the ocean providing habitats to fish and other microorganisms. The concrete used in forming the reef balls in pH neutral. The ball is hollow, and the surface is highly texturized allowing all sorts of creatures to nest and create a home. Growth can be seen in as little as a couple of weeks, and it will help support marine habitats for a lifetime.

Diamond

Several companies will take the ashes from loved ones and turn them into precious stones. They separate the carbon, and under extreme heat, they turn the carbon into graphite. Once it's been turned into graphite, they heat it again and put it under enough pressure to turn it into a precious stone.

95. Going Zero Waste and the People Around You

It's really hard to go zero waste and stay motivated when your partner is not on board. But I really want to encourage you to stick with it.

Can you imagine if out of the blue your partner came home and said, "Honey, I've decided I want to stop making trash." Kinda weird, right? Like where did this normal person go, and what Kool-Aid have they been drinking?

I get it; I totally get it.

It takes time for people to adjust. You didn't make the decision to go zero waste in one moment. You probably thought about it. It took a couple of articles about zero waste, maybe a book, learning about the health benefits, the cost savings, and looking at the package-free stuff in your town before deciding to go all in.

The keys to helping your partner understand zero waste or any lifestyle change are time, patience, respect, and kindness. You have to lead by example because this is *your* choice and no one else's. You have to focus on being yourself and doing your thing. You can only control your decisions. You can't get wrapped up in worrying about things you can't change, or you'll drive yourself and everyone around you crazy.

When you lead by example, you'll notice others around you starting to make small changes. The key isn't to force them into it. Just do your thing. I promise, people are watching.

If friends, family, or co-workers are rude or make snide remarks about your efforts, that can be really discouraging, but don't let them get to you. I've found the best way to speak to them is to really emphasize the selfish aspect of it. For instance, "I'm doing this because *I* feel better, because *I'm* eating healthier, because *I'm* saving money."

When people are snippy, they're often in a bad mood, or they feel like you're judging them. Even if you're not judging them, they're afraid that what they're doing isn't considered good enough. When you take your viewpoint from selfless, i.e. I'm doing this *for* the environment, to selfish, i.e. I'm doing this for *me,* people are much more receptive.

Then it's all about authentically living your values. You will be surprised how many people will approach you to ask you about your cloth bags or glass containers in the grocery store or at the farmers' market! These small conversations are great ways to help educate strangers about plastic pollution in a non-confrontational kind of way! Who knows, they may just get involved in zero-waste living, too.

96. Find Community

Whether your partner is supportive or not, it's nice to have an outside group of people who understand what you're going through. The zero-waste community is so supportive. You can draw inspiration, challenge yourself with new ideas, and even find some new friends that understand the journey and the process. They'll be excited for you when you find a new bulk store, and be sad with you when you get a straw in your drink even after you specifically asked for "No straw!"

Social media is a great tool to connect like-minded people. If you're on Instagram, browse the hashtag #zerowaste or my hashtag, #goingzerowaste. They're both full of amazing content. If you're on Facebook, look for a zero-waste group. You can use the search function to find large groups or even niche groups organized by city and state because finding a local community is even better! You can work on hosting clean-ups, encourage one another, spread the word in the community, and swap all of the best tips on where to find the best package-free goods.

Meet Up

A great place to look for like-minded friends nearby is on meetup.com. There seem to be meet-ups for everything! Just with a quick glance, I see a whole bunch of groups that have a lot of zero-waste potential. Groups like litter busters, foragers, zero net energy, climate election action, climate solutions, ecology leadership group, gardening, community building, and many more that aren't directly linked to zero waste, but they're definitely applicable and could go a long way in helping you meet like-minded people.

If you can't find a zero-waste group, plug into one that is similar. Once you start to build friendships and get to know the organizers, you can pitch zero-waste ideas for the group like visiting a bulk store, participating in a zero-waste DIY workshop or a litter clean-up, or even talking to city council about a straw or bag ban. There's so much that you can work to achieve! If zero-waste projects ever become more dominant, think of starting your own zero-waste meet-up where you can focus solely on those activities.

Neighborhood Apps

Once you've found a community through Facebook or meetup .com, try to find new members through a neighborhood app. Nextdoor is a really popular app in my neighborhood, and it's a great tool used to organize community clean-ups and tell neighbors about ongoing events.

And reach out to your neighbors—you never know you, might find a new zero-waste friend right next door!

Bring Friends!

Once the group is in the full swing of things, make sure you're publicizing your group. You want people to be able to find you and join your cause. Ask members to share the Facebook group with their friends. Ask them to post on Nextdoor or to bring friends to the meetings. The more public events you start hosting, the more your group will be in the public eye. If you're hosting a clean-up or another public event like a talk, make sure to send a press release to the local paper so they can include it.

You'll find that the more active you become in the community, the more people will want to join your cause.

Connect with Local Businesses

Don't forget to reach out to local businesses. Now, I know what I'm going to say might sound contradictory, but if you make flyers, it's nice to hang them in local businesses around town. I still think physical bulletin boards are a great way to get out a message.

97. Work Locally

Once you've found your local community, you can really grow as a grassroots organization. Many people put way too much focus on the top when really they should direct their focus toward their neighbors. The saying is, "Think globally; act locally." The way to actually see change is by involving the local community. There's so much you can achieve together at the local level, and it all starts with education and awareness. Once you understand zero-waste living, share it with others. It's not fancy or flashy, but it's necessary. Here are a few ways you can bring zero-waste living to your community:

Host a Clean-Up

Is your clean-up going to be a small group of friends or are you looking to go citywide? With a small group, you can get away with something really informal. All you have to do is call up your friends, show up with some gloves and trash bags, and figure out who's going to take the trash home to dispose of it.

If you want to host a larger clean-up, you'll have to iron out a few more details. Pick the location of your clean-up and figure out if it's a public park or a privately owned space open to the public. If it's a public park, you might need to get a permit through your local government office. If your chosen space is privately owned, you'll need to get in contact with the owner. They might even help you with the clean-up.

Next, pick a date and time for your clean-up. Decide if your event will be carried out even in rain or other inclement weather.

Create a flyer that can be passed around digitally and hung on local bulletin boards and in cafes around town.

Then, you need to gather supplies like trash bags, buckets, pickers, and gloves. You also need to figure out what's going to happen with the trash you collect: who's going to be responsible for taking it to be disposed of? Call your local waste management plant to see if they can help with the removal of the debris you collect. They might even be able to provide some supplies.

On the day of the clean-up, make sure the volunteers sign an agreement or waiver that protects you from any responsibility if someone is injured during the clean-up. You can also create a sign-up sheet to stay in touch with everyone who participates, letting them know about new events and workshops that you'll be hosting around town.

Teach a Workshop

Mastered a few of the DIY projects in this book? Share your knowledge with friends, family members, or the local community. See if you can reserve a room in a community center or library to hold a workshop to share your new zero-waste skills. You can collect a small fee from participants to help pay for the supplies. When you teach others how to make their own products, they feel a sense of ownership and accomplishment and are way more likely to continue to utilize those skills and practice a low-waste lifestyle. Here are a few DIY ideas from the book that would make a great workshop material:

- Deodorant (page 87)
- All-purpose cleaners (page 108)
- Lip balm (page 94)
- Lotion bars (page 85)

If you're feeling extra crafty, try a few of these projects:

- Make cloth produce/bulk shopping bags (old sheets work perfectly!)
- Turn old T-shirts into no-sew grocery bags
- DIY Beeswax wraps (page 40)

If you love teaching others how to cook:

- Show how easy it is to make bread using just flour and water
- Make jam from local fruit trees
- Make kombucha
- Teach others how to use roots and stems. Check out the food scrap recipes on page 57 for inspiration!

If you love to garden:

- Teach all the ways you can compost at home
- Show how to regrow food from scraps. Lettuce, celery, and green onions are very easy to start with. Once you get to the base of the plant, place it in a cup of water on your counter. Replace the water every other day, and once you see small roots begin to form, you can bury the plant in soil and place it on a windowsill. The plants will keep growing, and you can trim off what you need.

Give a Talk at a Library or Local School

If workshops aren't your style, why not give a 30- to 40-minute talk on zero-waste living at a library or local school? Public speaking can seem daunting, but with the help of a simple outline, it can be less intimidating:

1. Tell us about yourself! (5 to 10 minutes)
   a. Who are you?
   b. Where do you live?
   c. When did you start reducing your waste?
   d. Why is this important to you?
2. What is a zero-waste lifestyle? (10 to 15 minutes)
   a. What is the definition of zero waste?
   b. Why should it be important to everyone?
   c. What are the goals of this movement and what information will everyone be leaving with today?
      i. Some great takeaways could include five ways to reduce your trash today, more information about the local recycling and composting programs in your town, how to shop in bulk, where local bulk stores and vendors are located, or just a general overview of zero-waste living.
3. Talk about your specific topic. This could be a mix of all of the issues talked about in this book or just focus on a few key areas. (15 to 30 minutes)
4. Close out with a call to action. What's the most important thing people should take away from your talk?
5. Provide your contact information, so people know how to contact you if they have any questions. Don't forget to collect their contact information too! This way you can create a group of like-minded people to call on for the next time you host a clean-up or community workshop.

Ask Local Restaurants to Sign a Request-Only Pledge

Contact local restaurant owners about their plastic straw policy. This is an easy way to introduce low-waste ideas to businesses because it will save the restaurateur money *and* reduce the amount of plastic waste headed to the landfill—everyone's a winner!

Just to be clear, this is not a ban on all straws, it's simply the practice of providing drinks without straws unless a customer requests one. Most of the time people won't ask for a straw if they're not given one to start with, but it still allows for plastic straws to be available to those who need to use straws for accessibility.

Here's a sample email you can use, just plug-in your own information:

Good morning,

*I hope you're doing well. **Diner Town** is one of my favorite places to grab lunch—the **pecan pie** is my absolute fave! During my last visit, I couldn't help but notice that plastic straws are automatically provided with all drinks.*

Straws and single-use plastic, in general, have received a lot of media attention lately, for good reason. Currently, 8 million tons of plastic ends up in our oceans every year. Most of that is single-use plastic, such as straws, which is responsible for killing more than 100,000 marine animals annually.

Straws may seem small, but they add up. In the US alone, we use 500 million plastic straws every day! Cutting back on our plastic straw usage can be a simple way to start cutting back on our plastic waste. France has done away with single-use plastic cups, straws, and cutlery, as has Seattle. Even McDonald's is looking for alternatives to plastic straws.

*I would like to ask **Diner Town** to adopt a straw-on-request-only policy. This means that straws aren't advertised or automatically placed into drinks. Instead, they are provided only* *when a customer specifically asks for one or for customers with accessibility issues who require one.*

*This will significantly decrease the number of straws **Diner Town** uses, which will have a positive effect on the environment and your bottom line!*

I really hope you'll take my request into consideration. Thank you!

Sincerely,

Kathryn

Ask Local Coffee Shops to Advertise and Incentivize a BYOC Policy

Once you've mastered the straws, it's time to tackle take-away coffee cups! Disposable products, like coffee cups, cost shop owners money. Try to set up an appointment with the business owner or contact them via email or letter to see if they would be willing to give a five- or ten-cent discount to customers that bring their own cup.

You can offer to help make signage to publicize the new policy so everyone knows they can save a little money by bringing their cups.

Bring People on a Zero-Waste Shopping Trip

If you have a bulk store in town, invite people to go shopping with you and show them what kind of containers to bring, how to weigh various items, and how to pay for and store them. If you don't have a bulk store in town, you can take them to a grocery store and show which foods have more sustainable packaging.

98. Get Involved with Local Government

A lot of people ask me, "What do you find to be the biggest zero-waste challenge?" I never have a good answer because living a zero-waste lifestyle is just about changing your habits. Once you've changed them, you don't notice that anything is different. It doesn't take any more time or thought; it's just simply the way you live.

Once you have mastered the simple swaps, it's time to tackle activism. This can be organizing work in your local community like in Tip 96 or working with your local government.

In order for zero-waste/circular-economy initiatives to succeed, we need everyone. We need individuals, groups, businesses, and politicians all working together to create lasting change. And it all starts with you!

Citizens must act so businesses and policy can react. When citizens join together to create group action, they put pressure on businesses, then together the businesses and the groups can influence policy change. Then the policy puts pressure on businesses which then puts pressure back on the individuals.

A great example of this is a bag ban. Local citizens decided they wanted their town to pass a bag ban. These citizens came together as a group to put pressure on local grocery stores. A few independent grocery stores decided to voluntarily participate in a bag ban. With local businesses and citizens calling for change, there was enough public outcry that the city council passed a bag ban. Which then forced ALL grocery stores to adopt the ban, which then put pressure on the customers to bring their own bags.

Local government is almost more important than the federal government. If you want to start seeing change fast, this is where you need to start.

Head to your city's website to learn about the city council members and the local commissions which advise the city council. You can attend their meetings and recommend projects they should undertake.

If you're trying to host a neighborhood clean-up, maybe the city can help provide supplies or publicity to get more people involved. If you're looking to get a bag ban or straw ban passed, a local commission can direct you on how to shape the bill, and really help you formulate your idea into an actionable task.

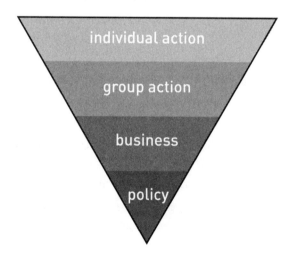

99. Find Personal Sustainability

A huge pitfall when transitioning to the zero-waste lifestyle is to try and replicate your old lifestyle. If you're trying to consume and live exactly the way you used to you're going to fail. In my pre-zero-waste days, I ate a lot of Pop-Tarts. I'm talking a box or two of Pop-Tarts a week. I would eat them for breakfast and snacks. They were one of my favorite junk foods.

When I first went zero waste, I thought I could keep up the trend by making my own Pop-Tarts. I was making 8 to 12 toaster pastries every Sunday for the week. It took at least 2 to 4 hours out of my weekend. It was completely unsustainable and exhausting. I was so focused on replicating my pre-zero-waste days when instead I should have been looking for easy, simple solutions. The harder you cling to the past the more time-consuming your life becomes. Instead of replicating what you used to buy, use this time to discover new things and new ways to simplify your life.

I find there's typically a thought process that goes with trying to replicate something mass produced that you love. It starts with, "WHOA. I CAN MAKE THAT!?" Then it transitions to, "Ok. That was fun, but I don't want to make it again." And it finally ends with, "There's got to be a better way!"

It's a lot of fun learning to make things you used to buy in a package. It's usually very easy and very inexpensive. However, once you start making everything, it becomes time-consuming. Making one or two things is pretty easy, but when you're making bread, mayo, nut milk, cheese, cookies, and muffins all on a weekly basis, it leaves you with little time for anything else.

You have to find your own personal balance, or what I like to call *personal sustainability*. Personal sustainability is so important, and it will look different for everyone—only you know your schedule, level of determination, and laziness factor.

For example, I HATE making tortillas. Words cannot even express the level of hatred I feel just thinking about rolling out tortilla dough. I cannot stand the uneven, wobbly sides, the hour I spend rolling them with a pin, and that I have to make each one individually. *Personal sustainability level: 0*

If something is that unenjoyable for you, you should find another way. What's so awesome is that in this day and age—there's always another way! I found a tortilleria right around the corner from the farmers' market that sells 25 tortillas for $2.00, and they'll put them in my own bag! *Personal sustainability level: 10*

To make things more personally sustainable, I always make a double batch of anything that can be frozen. I freeze baked goods in a cotton grocery bag. I freeze wet goods like cooked beans, soup, and stock in glass mason jars.

My next tip is to keep your active time to a minimum. You don't want to be in the kitchen all day long. I keep my active time to an hour including clean up unless it's for special occasions like holidays or parties. No matter what, it really boils down to doing what you love. If you hate doing something, it will never be sustainable. If you love doing something, it will always be sustainable.

Things you'll usually find in my freezer:

1. Loaf of bread
2. Chopped veggies
3. Veggie stock
4. Soup
5. Smoothies
6. Pancakes
7. Waffles
8. Bagels
9. Salsa
10. Marinara
11. Energy bites
12. Cooked beans
13. Veggie burgers
14. Meatless meatballs

CHAPTER TEN

THE BIG PICTURE

We made it!

100. Just Do It

Information overload can lead to analysis paralysis. Basically, you have so much information, you're not sure where to start first, which can lead to inaction. If you're feeling overwhelmed, start with the first five tips. They're pretty easy. Once you have mastery over those tips, then pick a new one.

I also want you to stay committed. When you're truly committed, you will likely encounter a pain point. For example, when I first went zero waste, I left my reusable grocery bags at home. I had two options. I could use the plastic grocery bags, compromising my values and allowing me to justify using plastic in the future, or I could go home and get my reusable grocery bags. I intentionally chose the pain point. I chose to go home because sometimes you need to feel pain to grow. It's just like working out, but here you're exercising your good habits. I have to say since then, I have never, ever left the house without checking to see if I needed a reusable bag. That one brief moment of pain was a lesson well taught.

101. It's Not about Perfection, It's about Making Better Choices

Zero waste can sound intimidating. That "zero" sounds so finite and harsh. It certainly doesn't help when you see people touting a mason jar of trash, and "all" of their trash fits in it for an entire year. The jar is supposed to be awe-inspiring and a conversation starter. However, it's not the goal.

It's also only part of the picture. It doesn't take into account any of the trash made in the waste upstream. The trash we wind up with is a very small percentage of the waste actually created. It's why it's so important for us to continue to push for systematic changes.

Going zero waste is not a competition. It's not about trying to "win" or see who can create the least amount of trash. It's about using your life and your actions as an act of protest against our current linear economy. It's about connecting with ourselves, others, and our planet. It's about living more in tune with nature and finding happiness not in our belongings but in the things that truly matter, like family, friends, and new experiences. In today's world, one of the most radical things you can do is find contentment.

Consuming less, repairing your belongings, and supporting your local community are all a part of the bigger picture. It's going to take a lot of people living by these principles to make a difference, but we can do it! We are doing it. There are thousands of people everywhere working to live a little lighter on the earth.

If you're ever in a situation where you feel down and defeated because you're not perfect, I want you to remember how awesome it is that you're even trying. You'll always have a cheerleader in me because any step you take in the right direction, is still a step in the right direction.

It's not about perfection; it's about making better choices.

ACKNOWLEDGMENTS

I started writing this book while I was working full-time in an office and working full-time on goingzerowaste.com. I would not have been able to do this without the support of my amazing husband, Justin. He was always there to go get takeout in our containers and keep the house in order, not to mention the amazing emotional support. There were days when things were hard, when things didn't go my way, when I just felt like throwing in the towel, but he always calmed me down, got me to take a break, and look at things with fresh eyes. I am endlessly grateful for you!

I also want to acknowledge the amazing zero waste community and the Ethical Writers and Creatives who've been nothing but supportive. I've found some of my best friends through writing and meet-ups. Thank you all for being a welcoming community and generally so kind, hopeful, and positive.

Of course, I have to thank my amazing parents, Gina and Jim, who've been so supportive! They are two of the best problem-solvers I know and always willing to lend a hand. I love you both so much.

I also want to thank both of the bosses I've had for being so supportive of *Going Zero Waste*. It's not very often that you find a boss (let alone two) who are supportive of your dreams. It's even rarer that they want you to leave your job with them and be successful. Thank you, Josh and Matt, for being amazing humans.

Thank you to everyone at The Countryman Press, but especially Aurora Bell for guiding me through my first book. And to my agent, Amy Levenson, who held my hand and helped me put together the proposal. None of this would be possible without either of you.

And, last, I want to thank my grandmother to whom this book is dedicated. Even though you're no longer with us, I know you'd be so proud. Every day I am inspired by you. You always supported my love for the theatre and the arts. We'd always watch classic movie musicals on repeat every Friday night when I was in town to visit. You were my hero and just generally the coolest person I have ever met. (Seriously, if we're ever out to coffee ask me about the parties she planned for Elizabeth Taylor or the time she gave away everything she had to dedicate her life to charity or the time she was delivering supplies for Food for Kids, broke both of her legs on the side of the mountain, got back in her truck, and FINISHED HER ROUTE before driving *herself* to the hospital . . . and that's just the tip of the iceberg.) I hope, in my lifetime, I can muster an ounce of your generosity and tenacity. A few short sentences can't do you justice, but I hope you know I am forever grateful for everything.

INDEX

ABOUT THE AUTHOR

Kathryn Kellogg is the founder of *Going Zero Waste*, a lifestyle website dedicated to helping individuals live a more holistic and eco-friendly lifestyle.

After a breast cancer scare at 20, she started questioning the products she was putting in and on her body and slowly started making changes for a healthier life, including avoiding endocrine disruptors which can be found in beauty products, cleaning products, plastic, etc. When she moved from Arkansas to California and saw all of the litter and trash on the streets, everything clicked. The products she was avoiding for her personal health were also bad for the health of the planet.

She wanted to start a website to help people make choices that were both better for themselves and the planet, whether they lived in progressive California or in Arkansas where they still had to drive their recycling into town. The goal of *Going Zero Waste* is to break down the concept of perfection. There is no perfect. It's just a bunch of people doing the best they can wherever they are, and Kellogg's goal is to encourage any change no matter how big or small.

Kellogg ran an experiment to collect all of her trash for two years, and the result fit into a 16-ounce mason jar.

She's been featured by *The Guardian*, CNN, *Martha Stewart*, Fox, NPR, and *US News*, and is currently the spokesperson for plastic-free living for *National Geographic*.

When she started writing this book, she lived in a tiny home in the Bay Area, California, with her husband, Justin, and their dog, Nala. She also worked full-time in an office. Now, they all live in a slightly larger home because tiny house living during your first year of marriage is rough, or as Nala would say, *ruff*. She currently works full-time from home and couldn't be happier.